T0354543

EMERGING TOWARDS APOSTASY

A DOCUMENTED EFFECTIVE ANALYSIS OF POST-MODERN, EVANGELICAL, AND PATRISTIC INFLUENCES UPON DEPARTING CHURCHES OF CHRIST

RUSS MCCULLOUGH

FOREWORD BY: DAVID PHARR

Order this book online at www.trafford.com or email orders@trafford.com

Most Trafford titles are also available at major online book retailers.

Cover art credit: Martin Britton, Graphic Artist, Charlotte, NC.

All Scripture references, unless otherwise noted, are from the
Webster Bible, 1833 Edition, a public domain work.

Some Scripture references are from the *King James Bible,* a public domain work.

Some Scripture references are from the *American Standard Version of the Bible,* a public domain work.

Some Scripture references are from the *American Bible Union* version of the Bible, a public domain work.

Other Scripture references:

Revised Standard Version of the Bible, copyright 1952 [2nd edition, 1971] by the Division of Christian Education of the National Council of the Churches of Christ in the United States of America. Used by permission. All rights reserved.

Scripture taken from the *New King James Version*®. Copyright © 1982 by Thomas Nelson, Inc. Used by permission. All rights reserved.

Scripture taken from the *NEW AMERICAN STANDARD BIBLE*®, Copyright © 1960,1962,1 963,1968,1971,1972,1973,1975,1977,1995 by The Lockman Foundation. Used by permission.

Printed in the United States of America.

ISBN: 978-1-4669-9798-1 (sc)
ISBN: 978-1-4669-9797-4 (e)

Trafford rev. 10/17/2013

 www.trafford.com

North America & international
toll-free: 1 888 232 4444 (USA & Canada)
fax: 812 355 4082

In those days there was no king in Israel: every man
did that which was right in his own eyes.
Judges 21:25[1]

Woe to those who call evil good, and good evil;
Who put darkness for light, and light for darkness;
Who put bitter for sweet, and sweet for bitter!
Isaiah 5:20 (NKJV)

All we like sheep have gone astray; we have
turned everyone to his own way.
Isaiah 53:6a (KJV)

Professing themselves to be wise, they became fools,
and changed the glory of the incorruptible God into
an image made like to corruptible man . . .
Romans 1:22-23a (KJV)

Beloved, believe not every spirit, but try the
spirits whether they are of God . . .
I John 4:1 (American Bible Union 1877/1955)

---

[1] All Scripture quotations, unless otherwise noted, are from Webster's *1833 Webster Bible* translation of the Bible, a public document via *e-sword.com* ®

CONTENTS

A Prayer of Dedication

Dear Lord and Father of Mankind;

Accept this book to the glory of our Lord and Savior Jesus Christ, King of Kings and Lord of Lords whose Name is forever praised! May His faithful servants be edified and may His wayward servants be restored. May these words be spoken, and taken, in love. May the Good News of the Gospel move forward unhindered by anything false that may be in the hearts of men. May both the author and the readers remain humble before You now and forever more. May we all look only to Your Word for "all things pertaining to life and Godliness."

All in the Name of Jesus! AMEN

"When we asunder part,

It gives us inward pain;

But we shall still be joined in heart,

And hope to meet again."

—John Fawcett

Dedicated to the Glory and God and to the memory of my late parents Russell H. McCullough, Jr. (1919-1966) and Joyce T. (McCullough) Considine (1925-2007)

ATTENTION: Web sites are in constant change. I have referenced many quotations in the Webography. Since I began this work in 2006, a number of these references may have been deleted, moved or changed on-line. I assert on my honor as a Christian that they were ALL entirely valid at the time of authorship.

—Russ McCullough

A Note of Thanks

Acknowledging my gratitude to everyone who blessed me in some way or another for this now finished work is impossible. I know I will leave off someone's name. To that person, or persons, I apologize for my oversight.

First and foremost, I give profound thanks to God for creating me, sustaining me and granting me the gifted ability to research and write this work. God gave me a most loving and understanding wife, Nancy, who on a consistent basis woke me up in the wee hours of the morning and asked if I was going to sleep in my chair or go to bed like "regular folks." She is a woman and wife like no other. To my Uncle C. L. and Aunt Judy Taylor, along with their son and my cousin, missionary to Italy, Jeff Taylor, for their constant encouragement, I extend my eternal appreciation. Thirdly, I am deeply appreciative to my publisher. for taking on this work. There are inherent risks on taking on a new author, financial and otherwise. Thank you all.

I am indebted to a number of other people for nearly endless reasons. To my fellow elders, Sam Hollingsworth and Tony Spickard for their prayerful and spiritual support, to David R. Pharr for editing, writing the foreword and hours of mentoring a first time writer, to Diana Nelson for text layout and numerous revisions, to Martin Britton for designing the front cover artwork, to the various men for endorsing this work, to Terry Wheeler for his appendix on philosophy and kindly gifting me a copy of Drew Breese's informative book, *Seven Men Who Rule the World From the Grave*, to Lowell White who loaned me his copy of Berkley Mickelson's most helpful book, *Interpreting the Bible*, for his constant encouragement and feedback and for kindly reminding me to be humble towards others, to Dan Owen who introduced me to Walter C. Kaiser's monumental work, *Toward an Exegetical Theology*, and to Chris Holley and Jerry Weldon for many a conversation regarding these matters. Again, thank you all.

Finally, I would like to acknowledge the example of the urgency of the gospel by my late father, Russell McCullough, Jr., and my late grandfather, Clyde L. Taylor upon my life. Equally I would like to acknowledge the example of a love of writing and preaching by my late mother, Joyce Considine and my late grandmother, Georgie Taylor. This work is more theirs than it is mine. It would have never been written but for their dedicated love of God and truth. They have all now "crossed over Jordan" and are awaiting our arrival "on the other side," gathered "with that so great a cloud of witnesses."

> Wherefore, seeing we are also are compassed about with so great a cloud of witnesses, let us lay aside every weight, and the sin that doth so easily beset us, and let us run with patience the race that is set before us . . ."—Hebrews 12:1 (KJV)

To these, and many others, "Thank You!"

Russ McCullough

Charlotte, NC/November 23, 2008

FOREWORD

The average church member probably gives little thought to the philosophical choices that are influencing how the Holy Scriptures are being studied and applied. We grew up with the assurance that the Bible "means what it says, and says what it means." Of course we knew it had to be interpreted-understood correctly, but that just meant considering context, defining words, and observing grammar. We knew that some statements had to be understood figuratively and that opinions on the meaning of apocalyptic sections needed to stay in line with what we found in ordinary prose. But our confidence in verbal inspiration and conscientious common sense had no sympathy with those whose theology rested on fanciful interpretations or imagined "hidden meanings" behind the texts.

Controversies within and without were to be debated by comparing scripture with scripture. Sometimes texts were twisted and misapplied. Issues were sometimes pressed to extremes. However, God's word was to be the final authority. And "book, chapter, and verse" was supposed to settle it for everybody. Biblical authority, either generic or specific, was expected for every issue of faith and practice. We knew that there could be no other way that the

Scriptures authorize except through "command, example, and necessary inference." We were confident that the right way to apply the Scriptures was the same kind of simple logic that knows two plus two equals four.

There have always been digressions from the "faith once delivered." Much in apostolic writings warned of departures (I Timothy 4:1; Romans 16:17f; et al). When in our times "change agents" started pushing their agendas, we were ready to meet them in the only way we knew. We thought it would be enough just to show what the Bible says. If they thought their innovations were scriptural, let them produce proof texts, or at least argue propositions from biblical premises.

What brother McCullough shows us in this book is that a radically different philosophy of interpretation is making its way into the church. We have wondered why those in our brotherhood who have decried what they ridicule as the "old hermeneutic" never said clearly what hermeneutic needs to be applied. Brother McCullough's documentation unveils their secret. It's a hermeneutic that doubts that the Bible really means what it says, that rather it is to be studied for its hidden meanings, truths embedded so deeply that one must look beyond word definitions and even biblical events. Astonishingly, it is accepted that such an approach may produce very different "truth" for different inquirers, but even if they are contradictory, they are thought to be no less legitimate. It is interesting that resulting interpretations conveniently fit their predetermined social, political and ecclesiological agendas.

Russ McCullough is an elder at the Archdale Church of Christ in Charlotte, North Carolina. He also serves the congregation as their gospel preacher. His spiritual passion is for teaching and applying what "thus saith the Lord." His scholarship is demonstrated in the research that led to this book. The careful documentation makes it a valuable resource.

The apostle Paul warned the Colossians of the danger of "philosophy and vain deceit" (Colossians 2:8). Worldly philosophy goes through phases. But Solomon said there is no new thing under the sun. Ultimately it all has roots in Satan's hermeneutic in Eden: "You will not surely die. What God really meant was that 'you will be as gods." That lie is too obvious to miss, but though dressed in more sophisticated philosophical clothing, its still the same false wresting of God's word, whether the allegoricalism of Origen, the tradition supremacy of Augustine, the imagination theology of Thomas Aquinas, or the hidden truth hermeneutic of Brian McLaren.

We are grateful to brother McCullough for his tireless research, and more especially for the boldness with which he defends what "thus saith the Lord."

David R. Pharr
Rock Hill, SC

EDITED BY:

David R. Pharr

PREFACE

The original title of this book was *Emerging Towards Departure*. I changed it to *Emerging Towards Apostasy*. The word "apostasy" is a deadly serious word. It comes from the Greek word *apostasia*, meaning REVOLT. There is a spiritual REVOLT within the churches of Christ. *Webster's 9th New Collegiate Dictionary* defines "apostasy" as a "renunciation of a religious faith." I prayerfully and reluctantly changed the title. I reached that decision to change the title in late May, 2008 upon learning that bro. Max Lucado signed the so-called *Evangelical Manifesto* at the National Press Club in Washington, D.C. His signature declares to the entire world that he has publicly renounced God's Plan of Salvation in favor of the folly of man. He is in open revolt . . . and not a word of this was reported in the leading brotherhood newspapers. I was stunned and dismayed but bro. Lucado had "crossed the Rubicon and burned the bridge." May 7, 2008 was a seminal and watershed date in the history of the church of Christ and we, as God's people, didn't even take notice.

The word "apostasy" has eternal implications regardless as to whether it is rightly or wrongly applied. Correctly applied, "apostasy" describes those who have abandoned the faith "once for all delivered to the saints" and embraced error, the kind of error that may drag souls into hell. If wrongly applied accusing others of "apostasy" makes one a focus of heavenly anger for wrong application makes one a judge of the motives of other men, a place God reserves for Himself exclusively. Erroneous application also makes one a merchant of "discord among brethren," a thing that God hates.

Sadly, there are now those in the church of Christ embracing and teaching "another gospel." It is a "gospel" built upon a foundation of neo-Gnostic interpretive methods, motivated by denominational Evangelical influences and propelled by pragmatic and self centered Post-Modern philosophy.

I often go to a web site known as *answers.com*. It is a great resource for quick reference material on most any subject. One night in the fall of 2006 I typed in "Restoration Movement" just to see what I would find. There was an extensive article on the churches of Christ. In the midst of the article there was a paragraph that puzzled me. The entry read: "Emergent Churches of Christ."[2] Frankly, I had never heard of the term. I then spent the next two hours reading about *"Emergent Churches of Christ."* I received quite an education that night. The purpose of this book is to convey to you, as objectively as I can, what I have learned since. I have documented this work heavily so that the reader can *independently verify* the validity of these assertions and conclusions in a Berean spirit. I will attempt to do so with gentleness and respect for the souls involved without attempting to judge motives. What you read here are not judgments of motive, but a forthright assessment of a movement among us. It's not important as to *who* is right, it is *what* is right that matters. "What is right" is that which is consistent with the revealed, clear and linear Word of God. With that in mind, my mission is threefold.

---

2   From answers.com/ "Restoration Movement/Churches of Christ (non-instrumental)/"Post 1906 Schisms"/paragraph #7

MISSION STATEMENT

First I intend to identify and bring to light an apostasy from the church of Christ that is philosophically flawed by Post-Modernism, spiritually flawed by Evangelicalism and theologically flawed by Patristic interpretive models.

Secondly, by bringing these issues to light, I prayerfully hope to warn the faithful of the dangers of the present hour and the dangers of the very near future.

Thirdly, by God's grace and mercy, I hope these words will encourage those who are contemplating a departure, and those already departed from us, to reconsider their decision and to turn back to the "narrow way that leads to life."

Finally, my primary approach, instead of examining the false deductions of these errors, is to examine the dubious road map to these errors. In other words, this work is an examination of the FOUNDATION of error instead of an examination of the CONCLUSIONS of those who are in error. There are numerous extant works examining the false conclusions of the Emergents, all done by those far more competent than I. Having said that, when we dialogue with the Emergents among us we will fail miserably unless, and until, we are thoroughly familiar with HOW they arrived at their erroneous conclusions. To that singular goal I give this work to you in the Name of our Lord and Savior Jesus Christ, the Creator and Sustainer of all things.

Thesis:

This work will show that those *Emerging Towards Apostasy*, are doing so by adopting Post-Modern philosophy, by becoming unequally yoked with denominational Evangelicalism and, most importantly, by adopting a Patristic and neo-Gnostic interpretive method based primarily upon the teachings of Origen and Thomas Aquinas.

SECTION I

POST-MODERN THOUGHT AND PRACTICE IS INFLUENCING APOSTASY

1. MODERNISM AND POST-MODERNISM

For some time I have noticed more and more congregations among us acting and speaking in ways that I simply just can't understand. It is as if some people are communicating in a completely different language! I must admit, I had no clue as to what is taking place all over the country. I now realize what is "going on" and here it is:

Many congregations have ceased to RESIST the culture and have begun to EMBRACE the culture, and some have even BECOME the culture.

What is "going on" is like something I used to experience years ago while listening to WGH, a 1960's Hampton, Virginia, "rock and roll" radio station, the "double play." The "double play" was simply playing over a song just heard. The song of today's culture is what we call *Post Modernism*. Post Modernism is, at its core, a "double play" of Judges 21:25 and Romans chapter 1 where everyone "does his own thing." The trinity that is worshipped by Post Modernists is "me, myself & I" instead of the Father, the Son & the Holy Spirit. As Solomon said; ". . . there is no new thing under the sun." (Ecclesiastes 1:9c) What I soon was to discover is what the late denominationalist scholar, Francis Schaeffer, discovered in the sixties, and that is, many among us are speaking a different language altogether.

"It is naïve to discuss the theological questions as theological questions until one has considered what truth means to the one making the theological statements".[3]

Sadly, some among us have a different definition of truth than they used to.

Before we can get a handle on how Post-Modernism has affected the Lord's church we must define the term itself. The scriptures just referenced, of course, render the best definition of all. Post-Modern man does just as he pleases, "king or no king." In fact the Post-Modernist crowns *HIMSELF* king as did Napoleon.

In the broadest of terms, Post Modernism is an "equal and opposite reaction" to Modernism. Until the 18th century, westerners, even when at war with one another over religion, considered

---

[3]   Francis A. Schaeffer, *The God Who Is There - Speaking Historic Christianity Into the Twentieth Century*, (Downers Grove, Illinois: Intervarsity Press, 1968, 1975) p. 51

the Scriptures the only source of truth, period. Before the mid eighteenth century, all westerners shared this same basic world view. Soon afterwards, however, the so-called "Age of Reason" was ushered in. This is what we refer to today as Modernism. Its premise was that man's ultimate truth is in his own ability to reason. It also stated that though the Scripture may hold "truth," it does not hold ALL truth. Thirdly, it stated that "truth" found in Scripture can also be located apart from Scripture as well. Modernism has left in its wake history's greatest tragedies. When played out in real life, Modernism brought us the bloodletting that was the French Revolution, Napoleon and what was truly the "first world war." For nearly 20 years Europe was engulfed in total warfare pitting agnostic France against the rest of Europe's theocratic monarchies. In the end, France was defeated but the Modernism that fostered the evil that was Napoleonic France, lived on. It was Modernistic thinking that led Darwin to publish the lies that will damn millions. It was Modernistic thinking that asserted that man has more "good" in him than evil. The Modernists liked to often mention the "divine spark," the idea that essentially "good" man can continually improve himself over time. In fact, the Modernists believed that man would someday reach perfection through sheer self effort. (Sounds a lot like Dr. Phil, doesn't it?)

5

Schaeffer wrote prolifically in the 1960's and 1970's about the cultural shift between what we now call Modernism and Post-Modernism. He saw this shift in watershed terms;

> . . . this change in the concept of the way we come to knowledge and truth is the MOST crucial problem, as I understand it, facing Christianity today. If you had lived in Europe prior to about 1890, or in the United States before 1935, you would not have had to spend much time, in practice, in thinking about your presuppositions . . . Before these dates everyone would have been working on much the same presuppositions, which in practice seemed to accord with the Christians own presuppositions . . . What were these presuppositions? The basic one was that there really are such things as absolutes. They accepted the possibility of an absolute in the area of Being (or knowledge), and in the area of morals. Therefore, because they accepted the possibility of absolutes, though men might disagree as to what these were, nevertheless they could reason together in the basis of antithesis. So if anything was true, the opposite was false. In morality, if one thing was right, its opposite

was wrong . . . historic Christianity stands on a basis of antithesis. Without it historic Christianity is meaningless. [4]

Schaeffer illustrates this shift by something he calls the "line of despair." Prior to about 1890 in Europe and prior to about 1935 in the United States, people thought in terms of having *convictions*. After about 1890 in Europe and after about 1935 in the United States, people began thinking in terms of having *opinions*. Conviction is static whereas opinion is fluid, changing and vacillating. Ever changing opinions are the hallmark of Post-Modern thought and practice. The bridge between Modernism and Post-Modernism was built slowly over a number of decades and was characterized by the destruction of conviction. This shift in thought as to how people arrive at knowledge and truth is sweeping and profound. Nothing remains the same as it was before. Before about 1935 in the United States people accepted the fact that there was absolute truth and that this absolute truth was revealed in the Scriptures, was understandable by the average person and was held collectively by society, even by unbelievers. Beginning about 1935 in the United States people began rejecting the fact that truth was absolute. Instead the false notion began to proliferate that truth

---

[4]   Ibid. pp. 13-15

did not emanate from Scripture, that truth was not understandable by the average person and that truth, if it exists at all, is held individually. As with any falsehood, permeation of the majority mindset is progressively downward. The shift is now complete as Post Modernism has not only reached the denominational world, it has reached the church of Christ. Schaeffer illustrates this shift as a downward stair step:

Philosophy

Art

Music

General Culture

Theology [5]

The shift spread in several ways: geographically starting in Germany, socially from the intellectuals to the middle class and disciplinarily from the philosophers to the theologians.

---

[5]   Ibid. pg. 16

Schaeffer's assessment is sadly correct. Though some residual Christian influence remains, American culture is essentially post-Christian. The Emergent church is a post-Christian church, it does not flow from the Scriptures. The post-Christian Emergent church flows from man's ever-changing and self-centered intellect.[6]

The illusions of Modernism were shattered by the senseless violence of the First World War (1914-1918). The wholesale slaughter of millions illustrated with chilling clarity that the assumptions of modernism were lies from the pit of hell. Mankind is not essentially "good" and he cannot perfect himself. A key component of Modernism, if not its defining one, is "Social Darwinism," a flawed theory that teaches that man is ever evolving upwardly through the "survival of the fittest." Denominational scholar Dave Breese observes:

Social Darwinism was fast (prior to WWI—RM) persuading society of a similar [to biological Darwinism—RM] conviction. It claimed that no problem was unsolvable, no difficulty unresolvable. Given time enough, all would be

---

[6]   Ibid. p. 16

well. Humanity had within it a potential that would not be denied. Let the naysayers and the pessimists be left behind, for nature itself had dictated progress and fulfillment, writing it large upon the bright scrolls of the future. [7]

Breese goes on to conclude:

> . . . (it) turned the early promise of the twentieth century into the greatest series of disasters the world had ever known. It (Modernism/Social Darwinism as defined by John Dewey) brought upon the world the greatest intellectual confusion, moral myopia, and carnage that has been seen in the history of man. [8]

The physical and monetary drain on the British Empire, for example, took her from being the most powerful nation on earth in 1914 to near 3rd world status by 1945 making clear this tragic truth. Modernism stole the soul of Britain, leaving her only the dust and rubbish of Post-Modernism. Prior to World War I, the vast majority of evangelistic energy, manpower and money came from her shores.

---

[7] Dave Breese, *Seven Men Who Rule the World from the Grave*, (Chicago, IL., Moody Press, 1990), pg. 153

[8] Ibid., pg. 154

Somewhere between "Flanders's Field's" and "Dunkirk," England gave up her belief in God. Today, there are more practicing Muslims in England than practicing Anglicans. Will people 50 years hence write that somewhere between "Pearl Harbor" and "Baghdad," that America gave up her belief in God? God help us! We must always keep close to our hearts Christ's rhetorical question; "When the Son of Man comes, will he find faith on the earth?" (Luke 18:8 (RSV) It is unfortunate that what drives society eventually drives mans faith. The tail does indeed wag the dog.

Theologically speaking, Modernism wrecked similar havoc. "Theological Modernism" stated that truth is found through human reason, experience and observation, BUT not by revelation or inspiration. However "lip service" is rendered to the Scriptures by the Modernists as having a "useful" role in society. Modernism is a world view that says that *truth is discoverable* but is ever changing and generational in its definition. Today's truth, though "true" today, will be useless tomorrow. When applied to theology the modernist would "accommodate" the scriptures to the present generation but would not bind those "truths" on subsequent generations. According to Prof. H. J. Ry, modernism says

". . . (that) faith (is) the experience of man's beliefs about God and not an intellectual assent to God's revealed Word" and that ". . . (the Bible) is not inspired by God and is not inerrant . . . Creedal formulas were true only for the age to that composed them.[9]

Phil Johnson, a noted denominational scholar, defines modernism thusly, ". . . at (Modernisms) very core and inception was an overt attempt to subvert and defeat the truth of Scripture with humanistic rationalism."[10]

Humanism has been around a long time, in fact, since the Garden of Eden when Satan promised Adam and Eve that they "would be as gods." The ancient Greek philosopher, Protagarus, came up with a philosophy now called "HOMOMENSURA," meaning; "man is the

---

[9] H. J. Ry, *Encyclopaedia Britannica*, 1968, XV, pg. 631

[10] From a lecture given at the 2006 "Shepard's Conference" at Grace Community Church entitled; "Absolutely Not!"—"Exposing the Post Modern Errors of the Emerging Church" by Phil Johnson. For a full text see emergentno.blogspot.com/2006/03/phil-johnson-critical-look-at-emerging.html. NOTE: Emergent Theology is so radical that EVEN evangelical denominationalists, such as Dr. Johnson, are very much alarmed. Noted evangelical denominationalist Dr. John MacArthur has recently released a book on the subject entitled: *The Truth War—Fighting for Christianity in the Age of Deception*. In this book I often cite denominational and evangelical sources to document my statements. I do so for this reason: If EVEN those steeped in denominational and evangelical error can see the dangers of Emergent Theology, HOW can we not?!

measure." In our time, as cited previously, the late Frances Schaefer said of this philosophy;

"Humanism is a philosophy that has both its feet firmly planted in mid air."[11] (Much like "Wiley Coyote" ® in the old "Road Runner" ® cartoons, I might add!)

Post Modernism, as a response to modernism, asserts that truth is elusive and not discoverable. Reason is no longer valid. Post Modernists continually "seek" truth but never find it either individually or collectively.

Truth seeking to a Post Modernist is much like chasing the proverbial "greased pig" around the barnyard. The chase is fun but there is very little chance of catching the critter, let alone holding on to him!

Here is where we have come historically, until about 1700 western man believed truth was obtained by Divine Revelation. From *ca.* 1700 until 1890-1935 western man believed that truth was obtained

---

[11] From a radio broadcast made by noted Reformed denominational scholar Dr. R. C. Sproul broadcast in late September, 2006 on WHVN, Charlotte, NC.

primarily by human reason. Today western man believes that truth is simply unobtainable, it's "each man for himself." Mankind has come full circle like the 1964 Glen Ford movie, *Advance to the Rear.*©

Based upon the quotations in this book, some of the most influential men in the church of Christ today are convicted of little or nothing, "as their foolish hearts have been darkened" by Post-Modernistic thinking and influences.

Post Modernism in its "purest form" is a world view where there is not a Creator God (or if He does exist, then He is an inactive, "retired," or a "Deist" God) where man is not subservient or responsible to any "god" whatsoever. The Post Modernist says, in effect, that since ultimate truth, even for this generation, is not obtainable, therefore, each person has the right to establish truth in his or her own mind. In other words, truth is ever changing, truth is in constant motion and truth is always individually defined. In the Romans 1 model, Post Modernist man becomes his own god and worships his own image. Since Post-Modernists themselves consider individual emotion as the ultimate definer of truth, they could NEVER agree on a single technical (objective) definition as just what Post-Modernism is! Be that as it may, here is how the online encyclopedia *Wikipedia* defines Post Modernism:

The term defies easy definition, but generally comprises the following core ideals; A continual skepticism towards the ideas & ideals of the modern era, especially the ideas of progress, objectivity, reason, certainty & personal identity, and grand narrative in general. The belief that all communication is shaped by cultural bias, myth, metaphor [allegory—RM] & political content.[12]

The assertion that meaning and experience can only be created by the individual, and cannot be made objective by an author or narrator. [Such as God—RM]

(Characterized by) parody, satire, self-reference and wit.

Acceptance of a mass media dominated society in which there is no originality, but only copies of what has been done before.

---

[12]   Post Modernists are uncomfortable with the term "cultural bias" so instead they embrace the term "narrative." A good working synonym for "narrative" is "mantra." [RM]

Globalization, a culturally pluralistic and profoundly inter connected global society lacking any single dominant center of political power, communication, or intellectual production. Instead, the world is moving towards decentralization in all types of global processes. [13]

Phil Johnson further observes;

Post Modernism is not a significant departure from modernism; it is just a similar attempt to subvert and defeat the truth of Scripture by glorifying *irrationality* [Johnson's emphasis] and portraying all truth as hopelessly paradoxical, ambiguous, unclear, uncertain, unimportant or otherwise unworthy . . . Post Modernism abandons the hope of finding any absolute or inconvertible truth, and instead, the Post Modernist looks for amusement by playing with words and language, and by questioning every assumption and challenging every truth claim . . . . in general (Post Modernism) refers to a tendency to discount values like dogmatism, authority, absolutism, assurance,

---

[13] See: wikipedia.org/wiki/Post_Modernism AUTHORS NOTE: Wikepedia is subject to constant updates and changes. This exact quote may no longer be part of this article at time of publication. RM

certainty, and large, commanding, exclusive worldviews—which postmodernists like to label *metanarratives*. ["... stories that people have used to define their place in the world."][14] Postmodern values would include things like diversity, inclusiveness, relativism, subjectivity, tolerance, ambiguity, pragmatism, and above all, a view of "humility" that is characterized by lots of qualms and reservations and uncertainties and disclaimers about whether anything we hold in our belief system is really true or not. Those are the very same values that are usually held in high esteem in the emerging church movement.[15]

In practical terms for this discussion, Post-Modern thought is *observed by this writer* as being characterized by the following, though incomplete, random list I have compiled over the recent past:

Truth is based on one's own subjective feelings.

Truth has no fixed values.

[14] The definition of "metanarrative" is from Karl Aspehund in his presentation entitled; "Extension of Self: Media, History, and the Perception of Style in the Post Modern Age." See uri.edu/hss/tmd/02k/Aspelundsummary.htm noted as a source on answers. com/metanarratives

[15] Phil Johnson, *op cit,* See Note #4

God, "if" He exists, is seen as subservient to man.

There are many paths to this "god."

All paths to this "god" are equally valid.

The symbolic triumphs over the rational.

The senses are to be trusted above intellect.

Truth is perceived, not revealed.

Convictions are scoffed at.

Opinions are honored since they can be changed as easy as a pair of socks. The Post Modernist is expected to change his or her opinions often as proof of having an open mind.

Tolerance is a virtue, in fact the supreme virtue to the Post Modernist, but ONLY as it applies to other Post Modernists. Total *intolerance* is manifested towards anyone not in the Post Modern mind set.

Success, as each individual defines it, is universally expected, nearly guaranteed, and can be pragmatically planned in advance. This is known as "outcome based" thinking.

Every inconvenience is elevated to crisis status. It was widely reported in the media on August 6, 2008 that a man called 911 TWICE because his sandwich was not made to his satisfaction at a local sandwich shop! The police arrested him for abusing the 911 service, shattering the man's Post-Modern presuppositions!

Truth is found primarily by one's own personal experience.

Truth is not static, it "evolves." (i.e. the Declaration of Independence and the Constitution of the United States are "living, breathing documents" and the intent of the Founders no longer matters, we can assign our own multiple meanings to these documents as it suits us.)

All stationary beliefs are to be attacked.

Feelings and emotions trump logic and reason.

Self Centeredness is king . . . "What's in it for me?"

All reality is perceived and individuals can "create" their own reality. (i.e. Making up one's own driving rules, "The Real World" on MTV & video games where "dead" players come back to life with the reset button are but three examples)

All opinions are equally valid, we all "agree to disagree."

Simply making a statement about something somehow "makes it so."

Narrative trumps facts.

Truth is "discovered" internally.

What appears to be external evidence no longer matters. (Have you ever heard the expression; "Oh, well . . . . !" or "Whatever . . . !" after undisputable facts have been laid down? FACTS are archaic and useless to the Post-Modernist. Sound hermeneutic principles are not only ignored, they are scoffed at when it comes to Christianity.) The old joke is no longer funny, "Don't confuse me with facts, my mind is made up!"

Mass Media is to be continually in use and not questioned in any way. (The evangelist of Post Modernism is "all things digital" and he preaches his sermons on our multitude of "electronic devises" on nearly a continual 24/7 basis!)

The pursuit of pleasure and the "good life" are paramount.

All pleasure is good and all pain is evil.[16]

Post-Modernism is not new, we have seen it before. What we now call Post-Modernism we once termed "existentialism." Existentialism is a philosophy (stretching the word!) that is literally built on insanity! It takes the constant ups and downs along with the continual internal civil war of manic-depression and weaves it into a world view! Existential "thought" turns the bizarre into the

---

[16]   As noted, this is a rather "random" list I have gathered. I have long been intrigued with how our culture, especially the business and political side of our culture, is obsessed with pragmatic and outcome based thinking and practices. Please write or e-mail me with any additional descriptions you can think of...OR...challenge me to remove any inconsistent with Post Modernism. For a more complete study, you may want to read *Moral Darwinism: How We Became Hedonists* by noted Roman Catholic scholar Benjamin Wiker. It was published in 2002 by InterVarsity Press. Though technical and difficult to absorb the work exhaustively covers the subject of just how 21st century Post Modern American thinking works. It is interesting that though the entire work is about Post Modernism, the phrase does not even appear in the index!

admirable, the twisted into normal, the irrational into rational and finally the unreal into a "new reality." Breese observes:

> The result of (Soren) Kierkegaard's emergence in the middle of the twentieth century can be described as theological and philosophical diffusion [contradiction is "truth"—RM]. Thinking moved from the rational to the irrational; reason gave way to feeling. Final truth slipped away, and the thinking of the world became a set of self-contradictions. Theological and philosophical diffusion— that is existentialism. [17]

The so-called father of existentialism, as noted, is one Soren Kierkegaard. Kierkegaard, was during his very short and disturbed life, called the "melancholy Dane." He lived in Copenhagen from 1813 until 1855. Instead of seeking treatment for his mental condition he celebrated it and, with his vast writing ability, attempted to "sell" his delusions as a "philosophy." His work had little effect outside of Denmark during his lifetime and he was not translated into English until a number of years after his death. His "philosophy" of despair did not really get a toe hold in the

---

[17]   Dave Breese, *op cit,* pg. 215

wider world until the close of WWI when the promise of Social Darwinism and Modernism came crashing down as a lie. Since main-line Protestant denominationalism in Europe had been co-opted by Modernism, the "church" had no answers and many fell sway first to the despair of Kierkegaard and then to the damnable lies of Marx, Engles, Lenin, Stalin, Hitler and Mussolini. Nature abhors a vacuum. When "Christendom" was removed from the soul of Europe, the vacuum that remained was instantly filled with the despair of existentialism . . . where it remains today. We are witnesses to the sobering reality that today Europe is in spiritual, philosophical and cultural trauma. Unless the church of Christ commits herself to the immediate re-evangelism of Europe we will soon view Europe totally expired on her deathbed, killed by the hand wringing "tolerance" of existentialism and the "noble ignorance" of Post-Modernism. Into this vacuum, instead of communism this time, will sweep radical Islam. Gordon Brown, Prime Minister of the United Kingdom has recently articulated a national goal of Great Britain becoming the world leader in *shiria law* compliant financing! Should America not turn from Post-Modernism, we too will suffer the same fate as Europe long before the end of the twenty first century. May God allow us all to have "ears to hear."

Visually, there is a precise picture of Post-Modernistic thought currently playing in the form of a commercial on T.V. You likely have seen it. The commercial is for a high end career job search web site called *ladders.com* ® In the commercial we see a tennis match. All of a sudden, the people in the stands rush the court and all begin to play tennis, each according to their own individually defined rules. Chaos, of course, is the result. The tag line says; "When everyone plays, no one wins." In a word, Post-Modernism is as Phil Johnson describes it, *"zeitgeist,* The Spirit of the Age."[18]

In the recent past some among us have attempted to "accommodate" the Post Modernists by implementing pragmatic outreach concepts. One such experiment is the so-called "community church." Community churches are, *for the purpose of this book,* churches of Christ who have discarded the name of Christ. This kind of extra-biblical outcome based thinking has led to "unequally yoked cooperation" with denominations in various social improvement projects. Such "cooperation" has blurred the lines between the "new reality" and the revealed truth of scripture regarding the biblical congregational model. These experiments, however, rarely *at the time* actually *embraced* Post Modern thinking as being biblically

---

[18]   Phil Johnson. See note #4.

acceptable for Christians *themselves,* but "the hand was too close to the fire and the hand was burnt."

Unfortunately, as with any surrender of conviction, there is not very often a "rewind" button. Eventually, corners are turned and we reach the point of "no return." Attempts to convert Post-Modernists have rendered the opposite effect, an open embrace of Post—Modernism by people professing to be Christians. A noted denominationalist, Haddon Robinson, has this to say regarding this syndrome,

> Of course in speaking to a secular world we dare not speak a secular word. William Willimon observed that some preachers seem to have bent over backwards to speak to a secular audience and have fallen in.[19]

As the now defunct ***Pogo*** ® cartoon states, "We have met the enemy and he is us!" This principle is illustrated in Patty Hearst, who was kidnapped by radicals a number of years ago. Over time, she began to identify with her kidnappers and finally joined them in their brazen crime spree.

---

[19] Haddon Robinson, *Biblical Preaching: The Development and Delivery of Expository Messages* (Grand Rapids, Michigan: Baker Academic. 2001) pg. 31-22.

Open embrace of Post-Modern thinking is now a real threat to the continued faithfulness of many among us. Many now identify themselves more with the Post-Modern "target audience" than with the truth of the gospel they had originally sought to proclaim.

In closing we must remember this: The Emergent church is Post-Modern and Existential. She has embraced darkness. The leaders of the Emergent church are disciples of the madman Kierkegaard. God help us!

But before existential Post-Modern thinking impacted the Lord's church it impacted the denominational world like a scud missile.

Section II

Evangelicalism Is Influencing Apostasy

2. DENOMINATIONALISM, POST-MODERNISM, AND EVANGELICALISM

Many denominationalists today are more "Evangelical" than "denominational," i.e. they identify more with a theological system than with any one denomination. For example, when asked, many people would rather identify themselves as "born again Christians" (THE overly redundant Evangelical catch-phrase so often heard in the media) than, say, as Baptist, Methodist, Presbyterian, etc. [Keep in mind that the term "Evangelical" has no practical reference to "evangelism."] This is all very confusing.

As discussed elsewhere in this work, from the beginning of the church until about the 17th century, Western civilization accepted the biblical premise that truth is defined in absolute terms and said truth is found within the Word of God. The Protestant Reformation took place within this world view that we will term as "Pre-Modern." The more "conservative" Protestant churches, known as "Reformed" churches, were and are "Pre-Modern." Though the Reformers draw false conclusions from the Scriptures regarding many things, they do accept without question the inerrancy of the Scriptures, as has every member of the church of Christ since the Day of Pentecost.

Though our culture is far removed from the Pre-Modern world view, many people are still motivated and defined by it. The late Vernon McGee, R. C. Sproul and John McArthur are all noteworthy Reformed scholars. The Emergent church is far removed from the Reformed church, in fact the Reformed church sees the Emergent church as its arch enemy. Emergent theology is not at all influenced by the Reformers. The Reformed church is Pre-Modern and is not influenced by Post-Modernism.

From the 17th century until the time of the First World War, the world view is known as "Modern." Modernism asserts the truth is knowable and discoverable but it is variable and individually defined. The Evangelical church is a Modern church, having "truth" but the kind of truth is more like *Jello* ® than concrete! Though the time of Modernism has almost nearly completely past, many people alive today are Modern in their thinking and in their theology. Modern Evangelical theologians would include most notably Billy Graham, the late Dr. Bill Bright, Chuck Swindoll and Pat Robertson, the late Adrian Rogers, Charles Stanley, *et al.*

Unfortunately, as of May 7, 2008, bro. Max Lucado added his name to what is now called the *"Evangelical Manifesto."* This manifesto has two aims, one is to "soften" the belief system of Evangelicalism to make it more accommodating to the new 2008 post-election political realities in the United States, and two—and most importantly—to leap frog Evangelicalism from "Modernism" to "Post-Modernism." Today's evolving Evangelicalism attempts to pitch a "big tent" made up of just about anyone who has "made a decision for Christ," [the "Sinner's Prayer" salvation experience] though Rick Warren [*Purpose Driven Life*] is now attempting to "straddle the fence" between "Christianity" and other "people of faith." Warren has one foot in the old Modern Evangelicalism and one foot in the new Post-Modern Emergent Evangelicalism movement. The pre-manifesto Evangelical church was Modern, the post-manifesto Evangelical church is Post-Modern.

An "Evangelical" is a "liberal Reformer." Orthodox reformers such as Luther and Calvin wanted to "reform" the apostate Roman Catholic Church but were not "totally back to the Bible" people *per se*. A Reformer could not be a Catholic and a Catholic could not be a Reformer. In fact, the Reformation sparked numerous wars in Europe that lasted for nearly 300 years until the final defeat of Napoleon in 1815. NOW, however, an Evangelical can be either Protestant or Catholic! The "liberal Reformer/Evangelical" no longer feels the need to reform the Catholic AS LONG as the Catholic embraces those things that matter to the Evangelical. On the other hand, this writer asserts that a *CHRISTIAN* cannot be Catholic, Protestant, Evangelical *or* Emergent. In order to discuss the "Evangelicals," we must first arrive at a working definition. Where did the term "Evangelical" come from?

> "Evangelical" was derived from the Greek word *"euangelion"* which means: Gospel or good news. During the reformation, Martin Luther referred to his movement as the ***Evangelische kirche*** (Evangelical church). Later, "Evangelical became a near-synonym for "Protestant" in Europe. It retains this meaning in Germany today. [20]

Open cooperation with these self proclaimed "Evangelical Christians" unfortunately exposed biblical Christians to an earlier Post-Modern misinterpretation of scripture, *i.e.* the error espoused by The National Association of Evangelicals, aggressively promoted by media giant ***Christianity Today*** along with the Dwight L. Moody Institute. Evangelicals often appeared with Dr. James Dobson on the daily radio show, ***Focus on the Family*** as well as with

---

[20]   See: www.religioustolerance.org/evan_defn.htm

Pat Roberstson on his daily television show, *The 700 Club.* The National Association of Evangelicals, founded in 1942, is dominated by the theology of the Billy Graham Evangelistic Association and is articulated by the teachings of the late Dr. Bill Bright, founder of *"Campus Crusade for Christ."* In 1956, Bright published a pamphlet entitled *The Four Spiritual Laws* which is foundational to the modern day "sinners prayer salvation experience," so called. [President Woodrow Wilson had his Col. House and Billy Graham had his Dr. Bright.] You can reference my web site, *www.sinners-prayer.info*, for a detailed exegesis of this false doctrine and its primary proof texts, all explored biblically and in full context.

An exhaustive attempt to define "Evangelicalism" could fill another book! For brevity's sake, we will settle for just two definitions, the first being a philosophical self-definition. The second definition is a more "real world" definition based upon everyday experiences and conversations of the author. Since Evangelicalism attempts to "unify" diverse belief systems, iron clad statements of belief are difficult to come by, though there are a few.

Gary Stern, an Evangelical blogger, posted in January of 2007 an answer to the question, *"What Makes One an Evangelical?"*

What makes someone an Evangelical Christian? Defining what it means to be an Evangelical has long been an issue of contention among scholars, reporters and . . . yes . . . Christians.

The Barna Group ® which does all sorts of Christian research, uses its own fine tuned definition. [It may be fine tuned but it is VERY similar to the official definition put out by the National Association of Evangelicals ® on their own website.] To be considered an Evangelical, one has to adhere to or believe nine particular points.

According to (The) Barna (Group ®), about 38 % of Americans define themselves as Evangelical. These are the folks the media refer to when reporting on the political and social influence of Evangelicals.

But only 8% of adults qualify as "nine point evangelicals."

The nine points? Evangelicals:

- Have made a personal commitment to Jesus.

- Believe they will go to heaven because they confessed their sins and accepted Jesus.

- Believe their faith is very important in their life.

- Believe they have personal responsibility to share their beliefs with non-Christians.

- Believe that Satan exists.

- Believe that salvation is available only through grace, not good works.

- Believe that Jesus lived a sinless life on earth.

- Must assert the Bible's accuracy.

- Must describe God as the all-knowing, all powerful perfect deity that created the universe and still rules it. [21]

---

[21]   See: http://religion.lohudblogs.com/2007/01/22/what-makes-one-an-evangelical/

Secondly, from this writer's observations, "Evangelical Christianity" is a unity movement among sectarian people based upon a "lowest common denominator" (author Michael S. Horton's phrase—RM) theology that unites people around:

- Watered down Calvinism, [22]

- The "sinner's prayer salvation experience", [23]

- Obsessive pre-millennialism and

- Blind loyalty to the modern state of Israel all wrapped up into a "personal" relationship with Christ at the expense of the "corporate" (the church for whom Christ died).

---

[22] NOTE: What I mean here is this: "Watered down Calvinism" is a salvation position more broadly defined by the Evangelicals than the Reformers. Evangelicals teach a much more generous "grace" than do the Reformers. The Evangelicals typically emphasize that a person, once saved, cannot be lost for any reason regardless of the heinous nature of their sins while the Reformed church emphasizes that heinous sin is a sure sign that the person was not "saved to begin with." Salvation according to Evangelicals is more generous than that of Reformers. A Reformer would see the "sinners prayer" as "salvation light." Evangelicals promote a "private" salvation experience while the Reformers promote one that is "public." Evangelicalism is "watered down" Reform Calvinism.

[23] For more information see: *www.sinners-prayer.info*

These items are readily observable by viewing Evangelical T.V. broadcasts, listening to radio presentations by Evangelicals and engaging in conversations with Evangelicals. The items noted above are what Evangelicals LOVE to talk about! Just ask one!

In Charlotte, N.C. where I live, I recently heard a radio ad for a reformed church that is attempting to oppose Emergent theology. It states; "We don't dumb down the Christian faith in order to market it to the marginally interested." [24] (It scares me when those in error make more sense than some of my own brethren!) Many Evangelicals, however, still cling to the idea of "Jesus, YES, the church NO!" These people make up the vast "stay at home on Sunday T.V. evangelist" non-affiliated church. Other than the above mentioned few "essentials," little else seems to matter to Evangelicals. They can be confessing or non-confessing, they can be charismatic or non-charismatic, they can be Protestant or Catholic, they can be orthodox or contemporary, just as long as they hold to these few core beliefs. According to denominational

[24]   This is from an ad that ran for a time for Sovereign Grace Presbyterian Church in Charlotte, NC. The ad ran on WHVN Radio, AM 1240.

scholar Michael S. Horton, "Evangelical Christianity" has a number of characteristics the most prominent of which is a "lower view of Scripture."[25]

Post-Modernists believe that ultimate truth is un-obtainable. The absurdity of such a position is striking. A quote from a blog called the *"Aspiring Theologian"* puts Post Modernism to the test with this rhetorical question regarding absolute truth: "Absolute truth does not exist." Really? Is that statement absolutely true? Or does absolute truth exist after all?"[26]

"Evangelical Christianity," under the influence of Post-Modernism, says that unity based upon a common view of scripture is NOT obtainable so everything other than the few core principles are simply thrown overboard. A "pseudo unity" is the sad result, having a familiar ring to the "unity" of the Tower of Babel. Presbyterians begin to look and sound just like Baptists who look and sound just like Methodists who look and sound just like the Assemblies of God, etc. We know, however, that God has given us, ". . . all things that pertain to life and godliness through the knowledge of him

---

[25]   From Michael S. Horton, *"What is an Evangelical?"* Article published in 1992. Currently on the web at geocites.com/HEARTLAND/9170/horton2.htm.

[26]   From *"The Aspiring Theologian"* blog site. See aspiringtheologian.modblog.com/

that hath called us to glory and virtue." (II Peter 1:3b) This same "pseudo unity" sentiment is now showing up among some of us. Later we will reference an address by bro. Terry Rush, the senior minister at the Memorial Drive church of Christ in Tulsa, OK who has sadly bought into this "unity at any price" philosophy. Long before, however, we began "sipping the **Kool Aid**" ® of Emergent theology," the denominational world downed it by the gallon. The Emergent church is 100% Post-Modern.

Emergent theology is about to split the Evangelical movement into two groups, the "here and now" faction of Brian McLaren/Rick Warren and the "here and the hereafter" faction of Billy Graham. Strange as it seems, there is a growing number of "agnostic" believers within Evangelicalism . . . and they want to take up residence in your congregation.

3. THE FOUNDATIONAL SANDS OF EMERGENT THEOLOGY

Emergent theology had more of an evolution than a beginning. According to denominational Evangelical Free Church of America scholar Grant R. Osborne, the 1980's saw a number of theological guru's begin writing about what was then called the "Post-Conservative" movement.[27] The term "post-Conservative" is generally attributed to a man by the name of Roger Olson. Along with Olson, Nancey Murphy and the late Canadian Baptist theologian Stanley Grenz all began writing about Post Conservatism about the same time.[28] All these writers came out of the already described Evangelical movement. Grenz is especially significant because Brian McLaren, a theological philosopher we will soon discuss at length, lamented his untimely death in 2005 as being to him a "mentor." He wrote quite a lengthy obituary for Grenz on his ***Emergent Village*** ® blog at the time. Osborne asserts that the foundation of the movement was a desire to "shift from battles over

---

[27]   Grant R. Osborne, *The Hermeneutical Spiral - A Comprehensive Introduction to Biblical Interpretation* (Downers Grove, Illinois: InterVarsity Press, 2nd Edition 2006), pp. 402-403.

[28]   Ibid. pp. 402-403.

the Bible, theological details and liberalism to a new constructive

theology that is more open to innovation and movement."[29]

Closely examined, the pseudo-interpretive dream of Grenz,

McLaren, *et al* very closely mirrors King Saul's view of God's very

clear directives in I Samuel 15 which is illustrative of all that is

wrong in the way that many are now interpreting Scripture at the

beginning of the 21st century. The clear Word of God was given to

Samuel. The same clear Word of God was given to King Saul. The

Word of God given to both men was identical, no variances, changes

or exceptions. That Word clearly, and without ambiguity, required

King Saul to "utterly destroy" the Amalekites.

> Now go and attack Amalek, and utterly destroy all that they
>
> have, and do not spare them. But kill both man and woman,
>
> infant and nursing child, ox and sheep, camel and donkey.—I
>
> Samuel 15:3 (NKJV)

How could King Saul misinterpret the above portion of God's

Word? God spoke a straight line, Samuel saw a straight line but

King Saul saw a circle. Samuel used linear methodology while Saul

---

[29]   Ibid. p. 402.

used circular. Linear interpretation asks the question, researches the Word of God, hears the Word of God and comes to a correct and verifiable answer. Circular interpretation, on the other hand, asks the question, brings up life experiences and emotional feelings, filters the Word of God through these experiences and emotions, comes up with multiple "truths" and literally manufactures its own "truth." King Saul changed the Word of God to suit his pragmatic plans for military glory and honor. When challenged by Samuel, Saul blamed the people and made up excuses. His circular defense utterly failed. Saul lost the kingdom to his rival that very day.

The way we interpret the Bible has consequences, potentially catastrophic ones!

Yes, the Bible teaches proper interpretive methods, illustrates said methods and shows us consequences of changing the Word of God. And yet, many among us are turning lines into circles.

The greatest challenge to the 21st century church of Christ is this; "Are we going to be Samuel or are we going to be Saul? Are we going to hear and obey or are we going to hear and ignore?"

I explore these issues regularly on my Biblical Interpretation blog, *http://samuelslinesaulscircle.blogspot.com*. Come pay me a visit!

We will explore the ramifications of interpretive systems latter. Below, I have summarized what Osborne notes as general characteristics of "Post-Conservatism" that soon evolved into what we now call "Emergent Theology." We will abbreviate "Post-Conservatism" with the letters PC.

- PC relies on experience rather than doctrine.

- PC is critical of Evangelical orthodoxy.

- PC is inclusive in matters of fellowship.

- PC is inclusive in matters of salvation.

- PC promotes experiential truth rather than propositional truth.

- PC states that truth is more found in a fluid rather than a static state.

- PC states that the Holy Spirit speaks, not just through the Word of God but equally through community and tradition. [NOTE: You will hear many among us who now embrace the instrumentalists "defend" a-cappella singing as a "tradition" and no longer defend it as "truth."]

- PC states that there is no "universal set of criteria for affirming belief."[30]

Osborne concludes, "So theology becomes a *conversation* [a BIG buzz word among the emergent (RM)] in which the community (and its tradition) reflects, reforms and delineates its belief structure into an integrated and prescriptive set of doctrines."[31] Post-Conservatism was the theory that soon became the reality of Emergent Theology with which we now must deal. It has spread like wild fire among the evangelical world and has spilled over into the Lord's church like a broken dike. While the Lord's church slept, the Emergent Movement began its institutional evolution in the early 1990's.

---

[30] Ibid. pp. 402-403
[31] Ibid. p. 403.

A telling insight into just how Emergent Theology has impacted traditional Evangelical churches is found in an interview by Andy Crouch with a noted emergent preaching team of Rob & Kristen Bell who "pastor" the Mars Hill Bible Church in Grand Rapids, Michigan, a 10,000 member emergent church that meets in an abandoned shopping mall purposely painted gray proudly proclaiming, as it were, the "noble ignorance" of Post-Modernism:

> The Bell's started questioning their assumptions about the Bible Itself—"discovering the Bible as a human product," as Rob puts it, rather than the product of divine fiat, [Kristen further states], "I grew up thinking that we've figured out the Bible, . . . that we knew what it means. Now I have no idea what most of it means. [32]

Previously cited Michael Horton sees several things as marks of Post-Modern Emergent Theology. These include;

---

[32] Crouch, Andy. "The Emergent Mystique," a posting on the *Christianity Today* website 11.01.04. See: christianitytoday.com/ct/2004/November/12.36.html

- "Leading Evangelical institutions doubt the Bibles trustworthiness and infallibility." [doubt by default . . . i.e. the scriptures are unable to bring about unity [RM]) [33]

- "Sermons are often "Pop Inspirational" rather than serious expositions of scripture."[34]

- "The electronic age has produced a new crop of God-man go betweens; i.e. radio, TV, phone calls, (websites [RM]), etc."[35]

- "Money and salvation have become intertwined around many of us. "They sell you salvation," sings Ray Stevens, "while they sing *Amazing Grace*."[36]

---

[33] Michael S. Horton, *op cit,* "What is an Evangelical?" - My point here is that "if" we cannot learn unity principles from the Bible then scripture is lacking in power. "IF" the Scripture is lacking in power in any way...it is not inspired, Christ is not raised, and we "above all men are most miserable." The evangelicals do not believe religious unity is possible so they have ceased discussing it, thus denying the power of the scriptures.

[34] Michael S. Horton, *op cit* "What is an Evangelical?"

[35] Michael S. Horton, *op cit* "What is an Evangelical?"

[36] Michael S. Horton, *op cit* "What is an Evangelical?"

Self esteem, self glorification, self centeredness (dominates [RM]) the preaching, teaching and popular literature of the evangelical world.[37]

The "lower view of scripture" that Mr. Horton refers to, as noted above, has several characteristics that now are accelerated to an even greater degree by Post Modern Emergent Theology which we will soon define. The Emergent church was Post Modern and Evangelical before it "emerged." Apostasy is a slow but steady process, error is progressive.

---

[37]   Michael S. Horton, *op cit* "What is an Evangelical?"

4. EVANGELICALISM, NEO-GNOSTICISM, AND CHURCHES OF CHRIST

"Emergent Theology" among churches of Christ, like its denominational cousins, is Post-Modern in thinking, Evangelical in practice and has "reconstructed a new reality" from our common faith and biblical roots. The fully emerged church does not look like, act like, believe like or sound like the faithful church she has left behind. She is so radical as to cause the faithful to wonder if we have more in common with some of our denominational friends than we do with these erring souls who are "going out from us." Sadly that assessment may be correct, though being "similar" and being "identical" are not the same thing. [38]

As with other departures since the 1st Century, "Emergent Theology" among churches of Christ is being copied from the outside. As noted earlier, "Emergent Theology" first showed up *ca.*1992 among Evangelicals who felt disenfranchised by their various denominations.[39] The most noted denominational Emergent

---

[38] See David R. Pharr, *"What it Means to be Distinctive,"* **The Spiritual Sword 39** (January 2008): pg. 31

[39] For a full discussion of denominational "Emergent church" theories see a book: Ryan Bolger & Eddie Gibbs, *Emerging Churches—Creating Christian Community in Postmodern Cultures,* (Grand Rapids, MI: Baker Academic, 2005)

activist is a man by the name of Brian McLaren, recently named by *Time Magazine* as one of the top twenty five Evangelicals in the United States. He has a web site that touts the Emergent view called **The Emergent Village**. ® [40] In March, 2006, McLaren attended a United Methodist Church conference in Nashville, Tennessee, where he stated the essence of Emergent Theology. He said regarding the movement;

> It feels like the church community in our society today is about a lot of things, but it feels like we're too often far away from the essential message of Jesus, *of compassion for yourself and your fellow neighbor.* [41]

We must grasp the significance of McLaren's statement in the light of Scripture. Jesus said that the *Greatest Commandment* is to; ". . . love the Lord thy God with all thy heart, and with all thy soul, and with all thy mind. This is the first and great commandment. And the second is like unto it, thou shalt love thy neighbor as thyself. On these two commandments hang all the law and the prophets." (Matthew 22:37-40 KJV)

---

[40]   See emergentvillage.com

[41]   From archieves.umc.org/interior.asp?ptid=2&mid=9040 [*Italic* Emphasis mine (RM)]

Note that McLaren says the essential message of Jesus is to have compassion (love [RM]) for YOURSELF first and your neighbor second. JESUS says that we should love GOD first and our neighbor second. Who's right? I humbly assert to you that Jesus is.

McLaren's view is so brazen regarding the "essential message of Jesus" as to leave God COMPLETELY OUT!

An excellent review on denominational emergent thinking and practices (provided in part by McLaren himself) can be found on a recent PBS ® broadcast on the subject. The reference will allow you to either read or view by link the entire story.[42] *[Compare what you find on the PBS ® broadcast with the public statements from the Kinetic Christian Church of Charlotte found in the final chapter of this book.]*

From here, things deteriorate further. "IF" McLaren does not promote a neo-Gnosticism, his most recent books are as close to such teachings as one can get. For the first time in 1900 years, significant portions of Gnostic teaching have seen a revival. Since

---

[42] See pbs.org/wnet/religionandethics/week845-and-pbs.org/wnet/religionandethics/ week846 NOTE: To view either clip, you must have RealPlayer ®

a good portion of ancient Gnosticism is not found in McLaren's theology, we cannot in good conscience actually call him a Gnostic. However, the Gnostic teaching of a "secret gospel" is very much a central part of McLaren's theology.

In fact, a book I will reference below is entitled *The Secret Message of Jesus—Uncovering the Truth That Could Change Everything.* [43] Both the title and the contents articulate manifestly this clear Gnostic premise. There is much written about Gnosticism but for the most part it is very technical and difficult to understand. However in May, 2006, the usually Emergent leaning *Christianity Today* published an editorial entitled *"A Faith Tailored Just for You"* in which a not so favorable picture of Gnosticism is painted.

Gnosticism taught that some people were special, with the potential to understand spiritual secrets that common folk lacked. Once you were let in on the secrets, it became clear that you were among the special ones. Before an evil demiurge (fancy lingo for "second-rate god") created the material world, a select few were endowed with a unique spark of divinity. This spark could now be fanned into a

---

[43]   Brian McLaren and Anne Ortlund, The Secret Message of Jesus—Uncovering the
         Truth That Could Change Everything, (W Publishing Group, Waco, TX, 2006)

flame that could be liberated from the flesh and rejoined with all the other sparks to reconstitute the true God.

> Gnosticism's attention to the little-G god in the human self feeds the egoism of the American temperament. This sort of thing has long been growing on our soil. Blame Ralph Waldo Emerson for watering the seed. Now, Dan Brown (author of *The Davinci Code*) and those who hype the Gnostic gospels are packaging it for people who haven't read Emerson. This popularized neo-Gnosticism, says New Testament scholar N. T. Wright, "declares that the only real moral imperative is that you should then be true to what you find when you engage in that deep inward search." The message appeals "to the pride that says, 'I'm really quite an exciting person, deep down, whatever I may look like outwardly." This endless exploration of the self, says Wright, is in stark contrast to the very Jewish message of Jesus, which focused on God's kingdom.[44]

In ***The Secret Message of Jesus: Uncovering the Truth That Could Change Everything***, McLaren teaches his brand of "plug and play

---

[44]   From christianitytoday.com/ct/2006/june/3.22.html; "A Faith Tailored Just for You"

Gnosticism," something we used to call "universalism," *i.e.* there will be people in heaven from all religions, not just "Christians," and that in even the most general definition of "Christian." Here's what denominationalist Dr. Gary Gilley had to say regarding McLaren's "ecumenicalism" in a recent book review:

> McLaren is sure the kingdom is populated by people from all religions, not just Christianity. It is open to all but those who actively oppose it (pp. 163, 167). As a matter of fact it is possible that some Muslims, Buddhist and Hindus might "begin to 'take their places at the feast,' discovering the secret message of Jesus in ways that many Christians have not" (p. 217). Of course, "there is always hope that we Christians will not be the last to rediscover the truth that could change everything" (p. 217).[45]

If salvation from sin is not the message of the kingdom, just what IS? According, again to Dr. Gilley, McLaren's idea of the message of the kingdom is vastly different from that found in the Scriptures:

---

[45]   Dr. Gary Gilley: svchapel.org/Resources/BookReviews/book_reviews.asp?ID=316

This secret message of the kingdom—what does it look like? In a word, "missional." It is a kingdom focused on injustice, poverty, education, integrity, the environment, hospitality, medical care, the healing of the earth, pollution, exploitation, greed, etc (pp. 84-89, 111, 141, 222-225). In McLaren's view this is what the kingdom is all about, not the redemption of souls . . . . In McLaren's program the spiritual barely gets a nod—the kingdom is all about saving the planet (p. 128). McLaren believes that if enough people catch on to Jesus' secret message this planet might just be rescued (p. 128) and even war will be no more (p. 160).[46]

The ancient Gnostic heresy taught a "secret gospel." This "secret gospel" was obtainable by only a few people who had somehow achieved "superior knowledge." The Bible, on the other hand, teaches us that, ". . . He has given us [ALL of us!] all things pertaining to life and godliness." In addition to his neo-Gnostic leanings, here is what McLaren asserts in his own words regarding other doctrinal concerns:

---

[46]   Ibid.

On Our Ability to Find Truth: "None of us has arrived at orthodoxy."[47]

On the Final Judgment Day:

> The phrase "the Second Coming of Christ" never actually
> appears in the Bible. Whether or not the doctrine to which
> the phrase refers deserves re-thinking, a popular abuse of it
> certainly needs to be named and rejected. If we believe that
> Jesus came in peace the first time, but that wasn't his "real"
> and decisive coming—it was just a kind of warm-up for
> the real thing—then we leave the door open to envisioning
> a second coming that will be characterized by violence,
> killing, domination, and eternal torture. This vision reflects
> a diversion, a return to trust in the power of Pilate, not the
> unarmed truth that stood before Pilate, refusing to fight . . .
>
> If we remain charmed by this kind of eschatology, we will
> be forced to see the nonviolence of the Jesus of the Gospels
> as a kind of strategic fake-out, like a feigned retreat in war,
> to be followed up by a crushing blow of so-called redemptive

---

[47]   Andy Crouch, *op cit.*

violence in the end. The gentle Jesus of the first coming becomes a kind of trick Jesus, a fake-me-out Messiah, to be replaced by the true jihadist Jesus of a violent second coming.

This is why I believe that many of our current eschatology's, *intoxicated* by *dubious* interpretations of John's Apocalypse are not only *ignorant* and *wrong*, but *dangerous* and *immoral*. [48]

Please don't miss noting that McLaren considers you and I . . . should we believe that Jesus Christ is coming again to judge the world . . . as *intoxicated,* as *dubious,* as *ignorant,* as *wrong,* as *dangerous,* and as *immoral.* More importantly, he blasphemes by referring to our Lord and Savior Jesus Christ as a jihadist.[49] As we point out in other passages in this book, this is the SAME

---

[48] See *www.extremetheology.com/2007/10/mclarens-everyt.html* quoting: Brian McLaren, ***Everything Must Change—Jesus, Global Crises and the Revolution of Hope***, (Nashville, TN: Thomas Nelson, Inc., 2007), pg. 144 (Emphasis added— RM)

[49] Please join me in prayer: Our Father in Heaven; We thank You and praise You for Your great mercy and patience with us. We pray, Lord, that Brian McLaren will have time and opportunity to reconsider these words, repent of his sins, confess the Name of Jesus Christ and be immersed for the remission of his sins. In Jesus Name, AMEN

Brian McLaren who lectures at Pepperdine University, who writes regularly for *New Wineskins* magazine, who often appears at various ZOE conferences and who was honored with marquis lecture slots at the September, 2008 "Summit Lectureship" at Abilene Christian University and the October, 2008 Lipscomb University "Preachers Conference." As I am writing these words, I remain mortified at even contemplating these watershed events. Peter, John and Jude would weep openly at such an event and so should we! Here are some disturbing McLaren quotes:

Salvation Quote #1: "I don't think we've got the gospel right yet. What does it mean to be "saved?" When I read the Bible, I *don't* [emphasis mine, RM] see it meaning, "I'm going to heaven after I die."[50]

Salvation Quote #2: "Most people think about the Gospel as "how to go to heaven after you die." But, is that really the Gospel?"[51]

Salvation Quote #3: When asked "how a salvation experience" looked to him, McLaren replied;

---

[50] Andy Crouch, *op cit.*

[51] Lynne Marian; "Conversations Count: An Interview with Brian McLaren," *Outreach Magazine*, July/August 2005. See christianitytoday.com/outreach/articles/counversationscount.html

Very, very rarely does someone have the date-and-time experience of conversion. Typically, a person comes to us because they're spiritually searching. They participate in our services, they get to know some people, build relationships, join a small group or maybe even start volunteering. And at some point, they connect with God. The Gospel makes sense to them. They know that God loves them, and they just say, "I'm in." [52]

Salvation Quote #4: In 2003, *New Wineskins* editor Greg Taylor (also employed by the Garnett church of Christ in Tulsa, Oklahoma along with Wade Hodges) interviewed Brian McLaren and asked him to discuss the "salvation experience." Here is what he had to say:

The fact that there are thousands and thousands of people who can point to an exact moment when they were saved, I wouldn't deny that for a minute. There are millions of people like that. But there are also many, many people who cannot. They either had so many different moments that were significant that they can't pick which one really marked them as regenerated or whatever. I'm just trying to acknowledge that you have both categories. Now in the New Testament, what's interesting, to

---

[52] Ibid.

me, is that the moment that seems to be very, very significant is baptism. So, very often when people talk about accepting Christ or being born again that's always based on an approach to evangelism—that really is pretty hard to find in Scripture. For example, the phrase "praying to receive Christ—I'm not against those at all, but I think we sometimes take an experience that really comes out of nineteenth century revivalism in America and then read it back into Scripture. And I don't think we should restrict the Holy Spirit to our own practices. I think we should just be glad for however the Holy Spirit chooses to interact with people and bring them to Christ.[53]

Note how McLaren in true existential and Post-Modern form can be FOR baptism and AGAINST baptism in the same quote! Not only that, he is PRO Sinners' Prayer and ANTI Sinners' Prayer in the very same quote.

We must pause here for a moment and note that such "double mindedness" did not originate with Brian McLaren! The thought process of Brian McLaren is very similar to that of the agnostic educator, John Dewey, of whom Breese has this observation:

---

[53]   From wineskins.org/filter.asp?SID=2&co_key=507 Greg Taylor interview with Brian McLaren in 2003.

The frustration of attempting to categorize Dewey is compounded by the fact that in the large number of books, essays, and magazines he wrote over the course of his life he dealt with topics in such a fashion that *he could be quoted on either side of most of the current arguments.* For him, nothing was constant, given, or finally true, but rather all things were pragmatic, adaptable, and subject to whatever interpretation seemed appropriate for the day and hour. [54]

Having said that, Dewey did not originate the idea of embracing the darkness of contradiction as truth . . . that dubious honor goes to a man we have already observed—Soren Kierkegaard.

There is no doubt that Kierkegaard confirmed and denied many of the same things. On one page, he seems to contradict what he has said on the preceding page. One reads Kierkegaard with compelling interest, but the frustrations of attempting to understand him go on and on. [55]

---

[54] Dave Breese, *op cit,* pg. 157

[55] Dave Breese, *op cit,* pg. 215

At best, Emergent theology turns ambiguity into an art form, at worst we realize that Brian McLaren has embraced the dark teachings of Kierkegaard and his disciple, John Dewey.

In the July/August 2005 edition of *Modern Reformation Magazine,* denominational theologian D. A. Carson summarizes McLaren's points made in his *Generous Orthodoxy* manifesto, explaining his theological presuppositions:

- Accept co-existence with different faiths gladly, not begrudgingly. It is not their fault if they are alive.

- Dialogue presupposes commitment to one's position, so it is surely not a bad thing to listen well. Dialogue should be congruent with confidence in the gospel.

- We assume that the dialogue takes place in the presence of God, the unseen Presence. In such dialogue we may learn things, as Peter does in Acts 10-11. Similarly, Jesus learns from his interchange with the Syrophoenician woman.

- Missional dialogue requires humility and vulnerability. But that should not frighten us, for when we are weak, we are strong. It is surely right, for instance, to acknowledge earlier atrocities committed by Christians, even as we remain careful not to disparage those earlier Christians.

- Each religion operates in its own world and therefore demands different responses from Christians. Christian witness does not preclude dialogue.

- The "old, old story" may not be the true, true story, for as we continue to grow, and even our discussion and dialogues contribute to such growth. In other words, the questions raised by postmodernism helps us to grow.

- Live with the paradox: we know no way of salvation apart from Jesus Christ, but we do not prejudge what God may do with others. We must simply live with the tension.[56]

---

[56] D. A. Carson, "The Emerging Church." *Modern Reformation Magazine*. "Faith a La Carte?" (July/August 2005 Issue, Vol. 14.4. See: modernreformation.org/dac05emerging.htm Here Carson summarized points made by McLaren in chapter 17 of *Generous Othodoxy*, pg. 256-266. NOTE: This is my assessment. With the possible exception of *Beowulf* and *Canterbury Tales*, this book was the most difficult book I have ever attempted to read. Thinking you have run a great distance, you

The "co-existence," the "dialogue," the "paradox" and the "tension" that McLaren mentions is nothing less than the embrace of the dark teachings of Soren Kierkegaard . . . *contradiction is truth.*

Brethren, this is nothing short of madness!

You may wonder why I have spent so much time speaking of Brian McLaren and his theology. Here it is:

Brian McLaren has had, and continues to have, expanding influence among "some" members of the church of Christ and he wants to extend that influence even further. He is bringing the dark teachings of the madman Kierkegaard to your congregation and mine unless he is opposed . . . and opposed NOW!

---

discover that you have run all day in a circle and wind up where you started, though exhausted and out of breath. Compared to reading McLaren, I am rested and relaxed after mowing my lawn on a 100 degree August day!

5. Emergent Evangelical Churches, Christian Churches and Various Kinds Of Departing "Churches Of Christ"

Under the influence of Brian McLaren, Emergent churches from Evangelical, Christian Church or former church of Christ backgrounds, seem to share several commonalities. According to *Wikipedia,* there are several general characteristics of emergent churches. They are:

- A flexible approach to and continual reexamination of theology . . .

- A belief in creating communities out of the creativity of those who are a part of each local body.

- A holistic view of the role of the church in society, this can mean anything from a higher degree of emphasis on social action, building relationships with the surrounding community or Christian outreach.

- Creative approaches to worship ["Will Worship"—Col. 2.23—(RM)] and spiritual reflection. This can include everything from the use of contemporary music and films to liturgy, as well as more ancient customs with a goal of making the church more appealing to post modern people.

- Use of the internet is a dominant medium of communication through various blogs, websites and on line videos.[57]

Several years ago "Emergent theology" began showing up among the Lord's people.[58] It was largely unopposed primarily due to the fact that "Emergent churches" seemed to opt for a low key approach until 2006, the 100 year anniversary of the 1906 U.S. Census that recognized for the first time that the self denominated Christian Church had departed from among us. During the summer of 2006, due in large part to the reporting efforts of the *Christian Chronicle*,

---

57 See en.wikipedia.org/wiki/Emerging_Church

58 Leonard C. Allen & Danny Gray Swick, *Participation in God's Life*, Leafwood Pulishers, 2001… and…Leonard C. Allen; *Things Unseen: Churches of Christ In (and After) The Modern Age*, Leafwood Publishers, 2004. (NOTE: LeafWood Publishers began as an independent publisher but "merged" with Abilene Christian University Press [ACU Press] on September 1, 2005. Emergent authors such as Allen, Atchley, Cope, Tippens, Shelly & Taylor appear to favor publishing under the LeafWood name. See leafwoodpublishers.com. LeafWood was founded in 2000 by Dr. C. Leonard Allen who continues as "Editorial Director.")

Emergent theology was front page news among churches of Christ, though it was not identified as such, as far as I can discover.

And yet, most Christians, myself included, until my encounter with ***answer.com***, could not even define "Emergent theology," let alone bring scripture to bear against it! And yet, God enjoins us to do just that for we are to; ". . . be ready always to give an answer to every man that asketh you a reason of the hope that is in you, with meekness and fear." (I Peter 3:15b)

Before describing the "Emergents" theologically speaking, it is useful to categorize the different kinds of "Emergent churches of Christ." At this writing, there appears to be no established words and phrases to describe these things. I have, for the purpose of this book, chosen terms and words to identify certain thought patterns, events and trends. Keep in mind, these are not judgmental words and phrases, but are used only for descriptive and assessmental purposes. Only God can judge motive.

First of all there are what I will describe as *"internally Emergent"* churches, people who on their own, choose to embrace Post Modern teaching. These churches can be driven to embrace what I would call "Emergence" by a larger than life personality "senior minister," and/or what I would describe as an "Emergent" or "progressive" minded eldership. The latter, *could be close* to what Paul warned the Ephesian elders of in Acts 20:28-30, that apostasy would arise from their own ranks. Secondly there are *"externally Emergent"* churches, people who are "planted" (a term freely used amongst the Emergents) by a third party to propagate emergent teaching in a "targeted" area, again a term freely used among the Emergents themselves. More on this later, there are substantial sums of money involved in "emergent theology" church plantings.

Regardless as to whether they are "externally" or "internally" Emergent, there are several "kinds" of "Emergent theology" churches among us. They are, again as I would describe them:

Pre-Emergent Emergent *Post*-Emergent

The *"Pre-Emergent church"* is one that is, as this writer would describe it as, having a "conversation" between two parties in an existing congregation that will CHOOSE to separate for, what appears to me to be, outcome based and pragmatic reasons.[59] Eventually, as it again appears to me, the "emergent" congregation will go off on it's own to become entirely "Post-Modern" while the remainder of the congregation will retain its traditional culture for those uncomfortable with Post-Modern trends. Sometimes, instead of forming two congregations these churches will opt for separate services, one traditional and one Post-Modern. Ongoing, we will refer to this phenomenon as "dual track identity," again a coined phrase on my part for description's sake. An example of this "dual track identity" is the establishment of the Post Modern Emergent "Gap Church" formed out of the Southeast church of Christ in Friendship, Texas. According to ***answers.com***, "The GAP is an expression of the emergent *conversation* gathering in the Southeast Church of Christ."[60]

These two churches, one traditional and one Post-Modern are linked in numerous ways but do not resemble one another in any

---

[59] NOTE: In the author's estimation, Emergent theologians like to use code words that will mean entirely different things to the Post Modernists than they do to the rest of us. In this example, the word "conversation" means a slow transition over time to adopt instrumental music and other non-biblical practices in an "amicable" way between two groups that were once one. In other words, a soft landing schism that is handled in an "I'm o.k., You're o.k." fashion. It appears to be an attempt at controlled chaos.

[60] See answers.com/Restoration Movement/churches of Christ (non-instrumental/Post 1906 Schisms/Paragraph 7/External links. *Italic* emphasis mine [RM]

substantive way. In other words, to the Post-Modernists, division over doctrine is no longer a thing to be avoided, it is to be, instead, *embraced*, or so it seems to this writer. It appears that these churches believe that they can denominate themselves and yet not become denominational. This thinking is contrary to the will of our Lord as He prayed in the garden;

> Neither pray I for these alone; but for them also who shall believe on me through their word. That they all may be one; as thou, Father, art in me, and I in thee, that they also may be one in us: that the world may believe that thou hast sent me. (John 17:20-21)

Sometimes, there seems to be Pre-Emergent churches that have not yet identified themselves as such BUT their preachers have their own separate web sites or "blogs" that ARE Emergent in tone and content. One such example is Wade Hodges' blog from Tulsa, Oklahoma. His congregation's web site has very few Emergent theology indicators, BUT Wade's blog has the tone and content of these indicators. Please read it for yourself, don't take my word for it.[61] One of the characteristics of Emergent theology is that often emergent churches seem to be in "stealth mode." It almost appears that these churches are not wanting faithful congregations to really know that there is a "conversation" taking place. Again, only God can judge motive. For clarification, as described earlier, I would also identify a not yet emergent congregation that has an emergent preacher as having a "dual track identity." That way, a congregation can be, for example, both FOR and AGAINST the instrument, etc. at the same time . . . or so it seems to this writer.

I would describe the *"Emergent church"* as one that *has had the "conversation,"* repudiated its spiritual heritage, and has openly endorsed Post Modern thinking and practices. An example of an "Emergent church" is the Northwest Church in Shoreline, Washington. This church is the result of a "conversation" held by an a-cappella church of Christ and an instrumental Christian church. They merged, dropped Christ from their named identity and embraced Post Modern practices. Here is their own statement from their own web site; "Northwest Church is a Christian church/

---

[61]   See wadehodges.com/Click on the right column topic; "An Emerging church of Christ." In a series of 6 parts, it is a "open window" to the thinking of, what appears to be, an emergent theologian. The text is rambling & tiring but informative.

church of Christ." Here is how their Sunday morning activities are described:

9:30 a.m.—Contemporary service w/ instruments

11 a.m.—Contemporary service a-cappella

6 p.m.—Modern instrumental service w/ a rock edge.[62]

Now even "IF" there were nothing wrong with instrumental music "worship," (and there IS much wrong with it), Amos still asks the rhetorical question, "Can two walk together except they be agreed?" (Amos 3:3—KJV) Splitting worship services along the lines of the instrument in the same congregation is not only un-biblical, it is institutional double mindedness and builds a "house divided against itself that cannot long stand."

Another example, I believe, of an Emergent church is the Richland Hills church of Christ in Ft. Worth, Texas along with its more Post-Modern church plant offspring, Bridgeway Church. Richland Hills is one of the largest churches of Christ in the world. Rick Atchley,

---

[62]   From www.nwchurch.net

the senior minister for Richland Hills, has now authored a book with the well known Kentucky based self-identified Christian Church preacher, Bob Russell, entitled *Together Again*.[63] This book sadly chronicles how some among us have surrendered their formerly held convictions on the use of instrumental music in worship.

[NOTE: I call this event a "surrender" as opposed to a "compromise." Surrender is when a party gives up entirely to its opponent, whereas a compromise is when both antagonists give up portions of their ground in order for hostilities to cease. With all due respect, "IF" these events are a "compromise," just what did the Christian Church give up in this "compromise?"]

Together Again is prominently advertised on the web site. Also displayed on its website, as of December 3, 2006, the Richland Hills eldership has surrendered even more ground by introducing a Saturday night "worship" service featuring not only instrumental music, but communion as well.[64]

---

[63]   Rick Atchley & Bob Russell; *Together Again*, (LeafWood Publishers, Abilene, Texas, 2006)

[64]   From www.rhchurch.org

[NOTE: See Appendix #2 for an analysis of 3 Rick Atchley emergent sermons regarding these departures.]

The Bridgeway Church makes the following statement on its web site: "Bridgeway is affiliated with a fellowship of churches that have roots in the American Restoration Movement, including churches of Christ and the Independent Christian Church."[65]

The *"Post Emergent church"* (also known as a "Full Expression Emergent Church") is one that as I would describe as having totally cut all ties with it's spiritual heritage AND has repudiated what she once held dear. One example of a "post Emergent church" is Crosspointe Christian Church in Ashland, Ky. The website **answers.com** states that Crosspointe is; ". . . (a) full expression of the Emergent church."[66] Crosspointe's own website states this; "Crosspointe Christian church is a dynamic new church plant, bringing contemporary worship to Post-Modern generations . . . *we are not the only Christians,* we are Christians only."[67]

---

[65] See note #2, answers.com

[66] From crosspointecc.us. *Italics* added for emphasis (RM)

[67] Ibid.

6. CHRISTIANS ONLY BUT NOT THE ONLY CHRISTIANS?

The statement; "We are Christians only but not the only Christians," is a very common mantra with Emergent churches of Christ. The phrase seems to have originated with the early Restoration Movement to let people know that New Testament Christianity was occurring in many parts of frontier America at the same time without organized connectivity. It also let people know that there was no one man or one group of men who were pushing any kind of personal agenda.

Unfortunately today, Emergent churches of Christ use this phrase in such a way as to infer that there are other Christians in other churches, *i.e.,* denominations. The FACT that Jesus established but ONE church is conveniently forgotten. The closest "justification" given for it's current usage that I have seen (cited by Atchley and Russell in *Together Again*), is that Thomas Campbell around 1807 referred to those studying the scriptures in order to COME OUT of denominationalism as "brothers."

[Seriously, whatever Thomas Campbell—a mortal human as you and I—said, inferred or didn't say has NOTHING to do with who is and who is not a Christian. As Christians, who we are and what we believe depends solely upon the inspired Word of God, nothing more, nothing less!]

As with the Patristics, we should cite Thomas Campbell for history and not theology.

One thing is for certain, however. It is an entirely different matter for people in the 21ˢᵗ century to study their way INTO denominationalism than it was for people in the 19ᵗʰ century to study their way OUT of denominationalism! Lest you think my statements too harsh, let leading Emergent leader Rick Atchley speak for himself. It is most ironic that bro. Atchley emphatically asserts in his first "Both/And" Sermon [68] (Approx. Minute 49), "The church of Christ is just part of the Kingdom of God! *They're*[69] not

---

[68] In a chilling prediction made in 1990, Breese states this in his closing remarks on the "father of existentialism," Soren Kierkegaard: "What will be the end of it all? It may well be that a new creative provocateur in the Kierkegaard mold will step into our midst and write another Either/Or. *THIS ONE MAY CALL IT BOTH/AND.* (Emphasis mine—RM) The point is that diffusion tends to create confusion, and confusion within a culture creates vulnerability." See: Dave Breese, *op cit,* pg. 223.

[69] He speaks as if he is not even part of the church of Christ!

the entire Kingdom of God." In fact, even more brazenly he makes the following wild statement regarding the use of the instrument in his 2nd "Both/And" Sermon at approximately Minute 46, "Thousands have studied the Bible *INTO* using the instrument and NONE have studied it *OUT* of using the instrument." Without going into the detailed history of the instrument, organs were not introduced until the eighth century and then were used exclusively for court functions ONLY until many years later.[70] Not until the time of the Reformation (sixteenth century) was the instrument normative in Roman liturgy. Now, we know for a FACT that Luther, Calvin, Wesley and Spurgen, not to mention Thomas & Alexander Campbell, all studied their way out of using the instrument! What an incredulous re-writing of the historical record by bro. Atchley! This is but one example of how a Post-Modern mindset can "create a new reality"[71] if the facts just don't line up with one's opinions.

Among churches of Christ, the "Christians only/not the only Christians" mantra has been used as a slogan for at least 20 years perhaps beginning with a sermon preached by former preacher,

---

[70] Everett Ferguson, *Church History, Volume 1 - From Christ to Pre-Reformation* (Grand Rapids, MI.: Zondervan, 2005), pg. 370

[71] An example how "narrative" replaces "facts" in the post-modern existential mindset.

now elder, bro. Jon Jones of the Richland Hills church of Christ in Ft. Worth, Texas. This, again, according to Rick Atchley in his 2nd installment of his "Both/And" sermons that introduced the instrument and Saturday communion at the Richland Hills church. As noted previously, these sermons were delivered during December, 2006.[72] The use of this slogan "appears" to allow congregations to identify themselves as Emergent to each other without faithful congregations discovering the fact until it is too late. As faithful Christians we must ask the obvious question; "If Christ established but one church and God adds people to it as they are being saved, when and how did God change His mind by adding saved people to multiple churches?" We would also have to ask a follow up question; "If God is now adding people to multiple churches, which ones are they and how can we find out where they are?" We then, or course, would be led to ask a final question; "If God is now adding people to denominational churches, why don't we just sell all our buildings, disband and throw in with anyone we choose based upon whatever whim is fashionable at the time?" There are certainly churches out there with finer buildings, more sophisticated programs and much more money than we have!

---

[72] From rhchurch.org/praise/Both-And_Church.html "Both/And" Part 1 @ approx. 53 minutes, 11 seconds.

Sadly, this mantra is just another way for some to assert that there may not even be a "church of Christ" in their view. The recent words of bro. Rick Atchley should bring us all to tears. As much as it pains me to quote this passage, here is what he concludes near the end of his 3rd "Both/And" sermon:

> The kingdom of God is larger than the churches of Christ, always has been, always will be. If God has determined that churches of Christ have served their purpose and that it is His will that *they* not exist in generations to come, that's His call. But I must say this right now, at least from where I see things, I don't see how God is honored by dying irrelevant churches. (Emphasis mine—RM) [73]

Note that bro. Atchley speaks of Christ's dear body as "they." He does not even identify himself as part of that body, otherwise he would have used the word "we." The sign on the Richland Hills building still reads "Church of Christ" but does bro. Atchley consider himself still a member of said church? If his carefully chosen words are any indication, he does not. This is what a *deconstructed* and *reconstructed* church looks like as an end result.

---

[73]   Ibid. "Both/And" Part 3 @ approx. 51 minutes, 2 seconds.

The truth of yesterday is ridiculed and discarded. Afterwards upon the ashes, error is constructed, enshrined and institutionalized.

Another, close to home, example of a "Post Emergent church" is "Oak Hill Church" in San Antonio, Texas. Once a congregation of the church of Christ, it has now "fully expressed its emergence" and now, not only uses mechanical instruments of music, its leader, Max Lucado repudiates baptism as necessary for salvation and openly embraces the "faith only" position of evangelical Calvinism. I write these words not TOWARDS or AGAINST bro. Lucado but FOR him so he might someday return to the faith "that was once for all was delivered to the saints."

On May 9, 2005 Michael Foust, who is a reporter for *Baptist Press News* interviewed Max Lucado. Here in part of that interview:

> *Lucado's church* is Church of Christ—but not a typical Church of Christ. For starters, *musical instruments are used* (although there is still one a-cappella service). Also the church has a *baptistic view of baptism—that is, that baptism isn't required for salvation . . .* Recently *his church*, which has some 5,000 members, even changed its name from "Oak

Hills church of Christ" to simply "Oak Hills Church." When asked about baptism, Lucado replied; "We never taught— the buzz phrase is baptismal regeneration, where you *go into the water lost and come out saved. We never taught that . . .* There are those who have taught that baptism is necessary for salvation, as if baptism adds to the finished work of Christ. We have *felt* that baptism is necessary for obedience, but that baptism doesn't add to what Christ does for us on the cross, and doesn't add to what a person receives by faith." When asked directly by Mr. Faust, Lucado replied; "I think I can say that I *changed my position"* to the question: "Have you ever changed your position on (baptism)?[74]

One note to add here, it actually seems that the Christian church side of Emergent theology is MORE inclined to hold to the necessity of baptism for salvation than Max Lucado is! Lucado's actions sadly illustrate the apostasy of some of those "other Christians," of which he is now one.

---

[74] Michael Foust, "Max Lucado Transcends Church of Christ Beliefs," in *Baptist Press News*, May 9, 2005. *Italics* added for emphasis (RM) I encourage you to read the entire article in it's entire context. "Google" the article title and it will come up for you to read.

Bro. Dave Miller speaks to these sad and verified apostate views:

> Another popular Christian writer, Max Lucado, expressed the same viewpoint [salvation precedes baptism—RM] in his book, *He Did This Just for You:*

> Would you let him save you? This is the most important decision you will ever make. Why don't you give your heart to him right now? Admit your need. Agree with his work. Accept his gift. Go to God in prayer and tell him, *I am a sinner in need of grace. I believe that Jesus died for me on the cross. I accept your offer of salvation.* It's a simple prayer with eternal results. (2000, p. 50, italics and emp. In org.)

> Lucado then followed this statement with a "response page" that provided the reader with the opportunity to make the decision that he (Lucado) had just advocated. The page, titled "Your Response," includes the statement, "I believe that Jesus Christ is the Son of the Living God. I want him to be the Lord of my life," and is followed by two blank lines,

8

one for the reader to sign his or her name, and the other to record the date (p. 51). [75]

A surrender of conviction on the instrument lays a foundation of a surrender of conviction on salvation and as mentioned elsewhere in this book, error is progressive. Bro. Lucado's multiple meaning, circular theology, *sensus plenoir,* reason over revelation and imagination as a conveyor of truth interpretive models propel him further and further into error. The steering wheel and the brake, as it were, have long since been cast out the window while the edge of the abyss looms ever closer. Bro. Lucado has now, not only identified himself with the National Association of Evangelicals, he has become one of their *leaders!* According to **World Magazine** in their May 17-24, 2008 issue, seventy five leading personalities from the National Association of Evangelicals have attached their signatures to a document billed as the ***"Evangelical Manifesto."*** Those signing include bro. Lucado. Announcement of the signing took place at the National Press Club in Washington D. C. on May 7, 2008. The entire document can be read or downloaded from the internet. [76]

---

[75] See: *www.apologeticspress.org/articles/2285*. Dr. Dave Miller, Ph.D., "Is Baptism a Symbol?" *Apologetics Press*, On-line journal article, 2003, quoting Max Lucado, *He Did This Just for You*, (Word Publishing, Nashville, TN), 2000, pg. 50.

[76] See: *www.evangelicalmanifesto.com*

Among other points of creedal identification, the Evangelical signers pledged themselves openly to the assertion that salvation is by faith only. "Salvation (is) God's gift grasped through faith. We contribute nothing to our salvation." [77]

Should there be any lingering doubt concerning bro. Lucado's "conversion" to the Baptist denomination, doubt no longer. It is now public record:

> Max Lucado, often referred to as "America's best pastor" as well as a nationally acclaimed writer, speaker and senior pastor of Oak Hills Church in San Antonio, shared a message of hope at Beltway Park Baptist Church on Sunday.

> Lucado and his wife, Denalyn, were in Abilene (Texas) this weekend to watch and support daughter Sara, a senior at ACU, in the university's annual Sing Song production. Lucado initiated contact with Beltway's senior pastor, David McQueen, and asked to speak to the congregation.

---

[77]   Ibid.

"I asked Pastor David for the opportunity to come and express our deep appreciation to the Beltway Park body for the love and care they've given my girls over the years," Lucado said. "A parent's biggest concern is for the well-being of their children, and Beltway has embraced the college students of Abilene. I want to personally thank you for the heart this church has for these youth and university students." [78]

The following descending chart illustrates how Bro. Lucado's *"silence in Scripture is an accelerator to license in faith and practice view"* has in 15 years taken him from truth to error. Error progresses downward.

Mechanical Instruments Added to Worship

The Name of Christ is Removed from Oak Hills

Baptism Is Rejected as being Essential to Salvation

---

[78] Rebel Taylor, "Max Lucado Shares Hope With Abilene Congregation," *Abilene Reporter News Online*, 17 February 2008

Creed-Based Denominational Identification is Openly

Embraced

Open & Public Denominational Status Reported Nationwide

As often stated, I write these things as an assessment, not as a judgment. Max Lucado, by his own words, has entered apostasy. He is in REVOLT against the Word of God that he once lived by and taught others to do the same. We should all pray for his return to the truth. I pray that I might one day have the opportunity to urge his return in person. Bro. Lucado, please come home . . . .

The apostasy that bro. Lucado now embraces is what one finds at the bottom of an ice covered down hill dead end cul-de-sac named "Christians only but not the only Christians."

We now know that "Emergent churches" can be either internally or externally Emergent and that these churches can be either "Pre-Emergent," "Emergent" or "Post Emergent." We have also, along the line, hinted at their theological practices. Since very rarely do Post-Modernists appeal to an objective source (*i.e.* the Scriptures), it is difficult to get a handle on all of this. This is a movement that centers around individuals who hold ever changing opinions but I will do my best to describe the "theology of Emergence" in a later chapter.

One aspect, however, of the Emergent church that is NOT moving in all directions simultaneously is the availability of ready cash, and in large amounts. That source of cash is something known as "STADIA."

7. The External Monetary Influence Of "Stadia"

In regards to "STADIA" I rely heavily upon the "belief" statements issued by the Kinetic Christian Church of Charlotte, N.C., an "Emergent church" planted in 2005 by this organization known as "STADIA."[79] [80] The Kinetic Church meets in one of the theatres inside Concord Mills Mall, Concord, N.C., a suburb of Charlotte. This church is Christian Church funded but had, early on, church of Christ mentoring, an example of what I earlier described as having a "dual track identity." For its first two years of existence, bro. Jeff Walling (pulpit minister for the Providence Road church of Christ in Charlotte, N.C) was identified by the KCC website as their mentor, and one of their 6 leadership positions, none of which by the way, are identified in the New Testament.[81] As of June 6, 2008, no mention is made of this mentorship on the re-vamped Kinetic website, *www.kineticchurch.com*, or on the Providence Road website, *www.prcoc.org*. The Providence Road website features the now altogether familiar statement; "We don't claim to be the

---

[79] From kineticchurch.com The Kinetic Christian Church in Charlotte, N.C. is an "externally planted (by Stadia) theologically emergent church" that continues to hold that baptism is "an essential part of the salvation process." (KCC website)

[80] From stadia.com

[81] From kineticchurch.com

only Christians. We just want to be Christians only." [82] Just who these "other Christians" are is not stated or implied. Not only that, just on "what basis" these "other Christians" became so is also not documented. [POSTSCRIPT: In 2011 the elders at Providence Road purposely split the congregation into two separate factions, those who worship with a-cappella singing and those who conduct "will worship" with the instrument.]

I mentioned earlier that there are large amounts of money involved in "Emergent theology." STADIA, named for the measuring term used in the Book of Revelation, is a California based organization made up of Christian Church people and Christian Church money, in substantial amounts. STADIA is an arm of *Provision Ministry Group* (PMG).[83] PMG is a large organization that is made up, primarily, of STADIA and something called the *Church Development Fund* (CDF).[84] CDF is a $400,000,000.00 (four hundred million dollar) church finance business and provides funding for STADIA. As far as I can tell, there is absolutely no oversight by any eldership anywhere of the business end. Here's how a "church plant" funded by STADIA *appears* to work. [Please note

---

[82]   See: www.prcoc.org

[83]   From provision.org/

[84]   From cdfonline.org

that I am not an accountant and "may" not have complete grasp of how the money end of this actually functions.] For three years prior to a church plant four (or more) Church Planting Networks (CPN's) are formed. Each CPN, usually a Christian Church, obligates themselves to contribute to STADIA a sum just below $17,000.00 a year for 3 years. One of the four CPN's is Stadia itself in a typical church plant. This fund, after three years, will total approximately $200,000.00. STADIA will then fund the church plant to that same $200,000.00 level. This money, among other things, goes towards market studies, demographic target marketing profiles, software, etc., much like a purchase of a franchise in the retail world. Once the church is planted there is a mandatory "tithe" for, I believe, 2-3 years. Ten percent of the weekly offerings will go back to either STADIA or a 3rd party whom they would choose to receive it. (It's not clear from the website as to who potential 3rd parties might be.) Since 3/4 of the financial burden for a church plant is borne by parties other than STADIA and potential income from the "tithes" may greatly exceed their original $51,000.00 investment, the fund is "grown" to allow more and more church plants on-going. One final note on the financial side of external emergent theological church plants I have found NO instance of a STADIA affiliated church with elders and NO instance of a STADIA affiliated church under the oversight of sponsoring elders from another congregation. Just who is in charge and "who reports to whom" is totally unclear.

We must ask ourselves this question, "How can such a pragmatic and aggressively capitalistic approach to church financing ever find its way into evangelism, even among the Emergent?" The answer lies in how the Bible is interpreted. Dead men are still speaking.

SECTION III

PATRISTICAL INTERPETIVE METHODS ARE INFLUENCING APOSTASY

8. The Theology Of Emergence— Dead Men Still Speaking

Central to the thesis of this book is the fact that the false Emergent teachings of Brian McLaren, Alan Jones, *et al* are not possible without the theological precedence of Origen and Thomas Aquinas. Not only that, the allegorical and mystical teaching of Origen and Thomas Aquinas are not possible without the theological precedence of the post-exilic Rabbinic tradition and the Platonic and allegorical pragmatism of the Alexandrian Diaspora. The Emergent church is an empty shell but for the super structure provided by Origen's "multiple meanings" and Thomas Aquinas' "truth through imagination" teachings, the VERY SAME super structure that upholds Roman Catholicism. With that said, let's now look at the theology of the Emergent church. "Emergent theology," is characterized in an article in *Wikipedian.com* entitled "Emerging Church." Here is what, in part, is said;

> The emerging church or emergent church is a diverse, controversial movement within Christianity that arose late in the 20th century as a reaction to the perceived influence of modernism *(previously defined in Chpt. 1—*

[RM]) in western Christianity. Proponents of the emergent church *embrace post modernism* and call the movement a *"conversation"* to emphasize its decentralized nature with contributions from people of a *variety of beliefs.* The emerging church seeks to *deconstruct and reconstruct Christianity* as its mainly western members live in a post modern culture.[85]

(PLEASE read Footnote #85. It is essential to understanding this entire study [RM])

The "Emerging church" is a church that has been *deconstructed* and seeks to *deconstruct* the faithful where ever they are found. Once the faithful church is removed, then a "new truth" can be built upon the ruins of the old.

---

[85]   See wikipedia.org/Emerging Church. NOTE: *Italics* added for emphasis (RM) One component described here we cannot over emphasize and that is; the *"deconstruction and reconstruction of Christianity."* This is the Post Modern way; challenge every truth and create your own "new reality." This describes what the Emergents call the "conversation." This is why Emergent churches don't look or sound like faithful churches. They have torn down the walls of objective and obtainable truth and replaced them with subjective, pragmatic, outcome based thinking and ever-changing personal opinions. The Emergent church is ever searching for the truth but never finds it…and that's the way Post Modern people appear to like it, for it seems to them that ultimate truth is neither discoverable or obtainable.

As my Footnote #85 indicates, the *deconstruction* of clearly revealed New Testament Christianity is a matter so serious it is difficult for me to find the words to describe the gravity of the situation. The situation is mortifying for those who would *deconstruct* truth actually place themselves into confrontation with God Himself! Deconstructionism has a long and tedious history. German philosopher, Friedrich Nietzsche (1844-1900) taught that "God is dead," that there is no such thing as "truth" and that which appears "rational," is actually "irrational." Nietzsche was one of the first (Kierkegaard was the very first in my view—RM) modern age "Post-Modernists." Here is how Nietzsche defines truth:

What then is truth? A mobile army of metaphors, metonyms, and anthropomorphisms—in short, a sum of human relations, which have been enhanced, transposed, and embellished poetically and rhetorically, and which after long use seem firm, canonical and obligatory to a people: truths are illusions about which one has forgotten that this is what they are: metaphors which are worn out and without sensuous power; coins which have lost their pictures and now matter only as metal, no longer as coins. [86]

Nietzsche was more of a philosopher than he was a theologian, much as is Brian McLaren today. His dark philosophy turned out to be an important influence on both Hitler and Stalin and continues to be a driving force today among Post-Modern people who relish the illusion that there is no God, no truth and no "reality." Unfortunately, as we observed Schaeffer's "stair step of despair" earlier, error first influences philosophy, then art, then music and then general culture before it influences theology. Since error is progressive, corruption eventually shows up on the theological doorstep.

Moving from philosopher/theologian to theologian/philosopher we find the father of so-called "higher criticism," Julius Wellhausen. Wellhausen was a German from the state of Westphalia. Born in 1844 and living until 1918, Wellhausen, nearly single handedly, changed how the Bible was interpreted by main line Protestant churches.

---

[86] Grant R. Osborne, *op. cit.* pg. 483 quoting: Friedrich Nietzsche, "On Truth and Lie in an Extra-Moral Sense." In *The Portable Nietzsche.* (Edited and translated, Walter Kaufman/Penquin, New York). 1982

He held that . . . human reason (See the chapter on Thomas Aquinas—RM) was totally dependable and insisted that it was the Bible that could not seriously be trusted. He presented the idea that the Bible, far from being the Word of God, was in fact a sublime collection of human documents. [87]

Taking the thought further, Breese concludes:

(With Wellhausen) Christianity ceased to be a religion based on *divine revelation* but rather became a set of composite religious views anchored in *human reason.* Revelation was doubted and then denied, and rationalism took its place. [88]

Wellhausen made the theory of the so-called "multiple authorship" of the Pentateuch popular. He borrowed the "dual authorship theory" of Richard Simon (ca. 1678) and added two more. Wellhausen contended that at least four separate authors penned the five Books of the Law. He conceded that Moses "may" have been one of the contributors! His theory was abbreviated by the letters EJPD,

---

[87]   Dave Breese, *op cit,* pg. 91

[88]   Dave Breese, *op cit,* pg. 92

standing for "Elohim," "Jehovah," "Leviticus" and "Deuteronomy." This theory attacked not only the veracity of the Old Testament Law but Jesus Christ Himself for Jesus, on many occasions, quoted Moses . . . sometimes by name, "IF" Moses did not pen the Pentateuch, then Jesus Christ was not infallible and the entire Word of God becomes just another ancient story book. Wellhausen's foolish notions are a cornerstone of agnostic cleric Alan Jones . . . a confederate of Brian McLaren.

Should you think than no one in the church of Christ could ever take the position that Jesus Christ God Incarnate would ever speak error regarding Moses and the authorship of the Pentateuch . . . think again. Listen to the words of bro. Mark W. Hamilton, Bible professor at Abilene Christian University:

> My Deuteronomy commentary in the forthcoming [*The Transforming Word*, publication now delayed until sometime in 2009 according to the Mark Hamilton bio page on the ACU website] one-volume commentary from ACU Press assumes a seventh-century B.C. date for most of the work

(some being later) but concentrates on the theological and rhetorical dimensions of the text. [89]

Brethren, this is not just an exercise in simple semantics and personal opinion regarding some minor detail in history. "IF" bro. Hamilton REALLY believes this . . . he is calling into question the very deity of Jesus Christ himself! Think about it! "IF" Jesus Christ was mistaken regarding the true authorship of the Pentateuch, then He either is, was and shall ever be:

A liar and/or

A lunatic and/or

Mistaken

With all due respect to bro. Hamilton's research, Jesus Christ is NOT God "IF" he got the authorship of the Pentateuch wrong! I would think, instead, that bro. Hamilton has just read and studied

---

[89]   Mark W. Hamilton, "Transition and Continuity: Biblical Scholarship in Today's Churches of Christ," In: the *Stone-Campbell Jourrnal*, 9 (Fall, 2006), pg. 187-203 as quoted by: William Woodson, "Who Wrote the First Five Books?" in the journal *Spiritual Sword*. Volume 39, October, 2007, No. 1, pg. 12-16.

too much Wellhausen and Alan Jones. For an objective and scholarly look at this subject I would encourage you to read bro. William Woodson's article, "Who Wrote the First Five Books?" in the October, 2007 issue of the *Spiritual Sword*, pg. 12-16.

Jacques Derrida (1930-2004) was a theologian who was greatly influenced by Nietzsche. Derrida was radically Post-Modern. Osborne observes:

> Derrida attacks the very foundation of Western philosophical thinking, arguing that philosophy no longer holds an unassailable, privileged place as the overseer of truth. [90]

Osborne observes further on Derrida's views:

> Since Socrates and Plato, Nietzsche and Derrida assert, rational thinking has maintained a tyrannical hold over human understanding. Since all logic pretends to be rational but is actually metaphorical, attempts to determine meaning are doomed to failure, and truth is radically relative.

---

[90]   Grant r. Osborne, *op. cit.* pg. 482

Philosophy claims to be logical, but in fact it is rhetorical and so is both an illusion and a fraud. [91]

How just would Nietzsche via Derrida come together philosophically and theologically? How would THEY look at a Bible text? Osborne observes:

A text like the resurrection narrative of Mark 16:1-8 no longer has any connection with the original author or readers. It consists of a series of signs that draw the reader into "freeplay" in its textual arena . . .

What would a *deconstructionist* do to a text like Mark 16:1-8?

Deconstructionists would do two things to Mark 16:1-8. First they would radically reject the historical referent that ties the text to first century Christianity and would look for codes that unlock the narrative to new meanings. Second, they would delineate the multiplicity of new concepts that lay under the surface codes. At the level of original meaning they would detect nothing but "absence" and therefore would

---

[91]   Grant R. Osborne, *op. cit.* pg. 482-483

stress only the present interaction of the reader, who re-creates the text in newness. [92]

Other *deconstructionist* theologians have impacted interpretive theories in recent years. Few have has as much influence as Karl Barth (1886-1968). Like so many other Modernists, the senseless death and destruction of the 1st World War destroyed what little faith in God he had left, a faith that prior to the war was built upon the theory that via the "social gospel," mankind could continually improve itself until utopia arrived. Silva observes:

Liberalism, believing that the proclamation of a "social gospel" would bring God's kingdom of peace to the earth, had relied heavily on an optimistic view of human nature. Those hopes were crushed by the war . . . Soon after the war, Barth published a commentary on Paul's epistle to the Romans that sent shock waves through academia . . . Instead of focusing on the historical meaning of the text, Barth seemed to ignore that meaning because of his preoccupation with the *relevance* of the text for today's reader. [93]

---

[92] Grant R. Osborne, *op. cit.* pgs. 483, 485-486

[93] Walter C. Kaiser, Jr. and Moises Silva, *Introduction to Biblical Hermeneutics—The Search for Meaning*, (Zondervan, Grand Rapids, MI, 1994, 2007), pg. 275-276

Barth mentored a protégé by the name of Rudolf Bultmann (1884-1976.) As we have oft noted, error is progressive. Bultmann took Barth's obsession regarding "relevance" to the next level by injecting "mythology" into the already overly subjective influences of Barth. Silva sheds additional light on the views of Bultmann:

> If we moderns cannot believe in miracles, he argued, then we must reclothe the primitive Christian message in terms that are understandable to us. This principle led Bultmann to develop a hermeneutical method known as *demythologization* (but perhaps more accurately described as *remythologization*). He believed that the early Christians used mythical categories to give expression to their Easter faith. One must not think of myths as fabrications intended to deceive. Indeed, Bultmann's approach did not precisely involve rejecting the myths but translating them into modern myths.[94]

Many of Bultmann's followers today are running around looking for the so-called "historical Jesus," a Jesus that never existed . . . a "Jesus" that can ultimately be manipulated into a left wing political

---

[94] Ibid. pg. 277

activist. Both Barth and Bultmann, emphasizing "relevance" and "mythology" have led to the radical interpretive conclusion of theologian J. S. Croatto that humans can actually pour their own "meanings" into the Holy Writ! (Ultimately, we owe this radicalism to the "multiple meaning" allegorical interpretive approach of Origen and the "imagination is truth" theory of Thomas Aquinas as we will explore in detail in later chapters.) Listen to what Croatto believes:

> Croatto . . . tells us that the readers responsibility is not exegesis—bringing out a pure meaning the way one might take an object out of a treasure chest—but properly, eisegesis; that is, we must "enter" the text with new questions so as to produce a new meaning. [95]

Taking Croatto to the next level is German philosopher Hans Georg Gadamer. Have you ever seen the bumper sticker proclaiming the statement, "Question Reality?" That's Croatto and Gadamer, together like Sears & Roebuck ®! Gadamer infers that "truth in interpretation is a matter of personal taste." [96]

---

[95]   Ibid. pg. 279

[96]   Ibid. pg. 278

Whether an interpretation is true is a matter of taste. If this seems to denigrate truth, that is only because we have denigrated taste as a cognitive capacity able to arrive at the truth. It is only because we have thought truth is exclusively something that has been or can be proven. [97]

Error progressing from personal relevance to mythology to personal taste leads us where? In addition to anywhere we humans want to go theologically, the Holy Writ becomes . . . as it were . . . a Mao style "Little Red Book" demanding the imposition of Marxist economic models such as we have seen since 1959 in Cuba, Nicaragua and most recently Venezuela. This is precisely where Brian McLaren's theological theories have evolved. He blames all the world's ills on the "over consumption" of Western economies which, in his warped view, is the "true" definition of "sin" in the world. Should you think this statement "over the top," consider Brian McLaren's own words in an interview from October, 2007:

. . . there are people like Richard Horsley and Ched Myers writing on the relationship between Jesus and the Roman

---

[97] Ibid. pg. 278 footnote quoting Joel C. Weinsheimer, *Gadamer's Hermeneutics: A Reading of Truth and Method*, (New Haven, Conn.: Yale University Press, 1985), pg. 111

Empire. And of course, the Latin American liberation theologians have a lot of insight into Jesus and his context. For example, John Sobrino's *Jesus the Liberator* and Leonardo Boff's *Jesus Christ Liberator*; these were really phenomenal books for me. [98]

McLaren makes no secret of his admiration of his "liberation theology" colleagues. Liberation theology saw its rise in the early 1980's in Central and South America. It manifested itself primarily among agnostic leaning Roman Catholic clerics. Che Guevara was the movements chief martyr and saint. Breese gives us a good summary of the movement:

Liberation theology advances another fascinating rationale. In that possessing money is the essence of sin, it follows that the most sinful system in the world is capitalism. The liberationists then ask, "From whence does capitalism come?" The answer is, of course, the United States. For the liberationist, then, the sinful system is capitalism, the iniquitous nation is America, and the great Satan of the

---

[98] See *The Other Journal*, on-line blog for Mars Hill Seminary. Jon Stanley, *"Everything Must Change*, A Conversation with Brian McLaren. Link: http://www.theotherjournal.com/article.php?id=255

world is the President of the United States [regardless as to which political party—RM]. Most interestingly, by these twists of logic liberation theology joins the Marxist cause and advocates the overthrow of the United States—and for that matter, Christian civilization—in the coming Marxist revolution. [99]

How could Brian McLaren, even with his circular interpretive models, come to such radicalism? Observe this quote regarding the "interpretation" of Genesis from McLaren out of his 2007 socialist manifesto, *Everything Must Change—Jesus, Global Crises and the Revolution of Hope:*

It's interesting to consider the importance of consumption in the biblical narrative. When the crisis of human evil is introduced in a passage beginning in Genesis 1:19 and ending in 2:20, forms of the words "eat" and "food" are used about twenty times. Consumption is closely linked with human evil. Adam and Eve live in harmony with creation in a garden, surrounded by food-bearing trees. But to be a human being is to live within creaturely limits in God's

---

[99]   Dave Breese, *op cit,* pg. 86

creation—reflected in self-restraint in regard to eating the fruit of 'the knowledge of good and evil' (Genesis 2:17). If they break the limits represented by the fruit hanging on that tree, they will taste death (or as we said earlier, they will decompose).

Eve exceeds the limit, drawn to consume a fruit that "was good for food and was pleasing to the eye, and also desirable for gaining wisdom" (3:6). Adam joins her. As a result, an avalanche of alienation crashes into the human story— alienation from God, alienation from one another, alienation from oneself, and alienation from the creation.

In the following chapters, brother is alienated from brother and a form of class violence enters the story, as the class of pastoralists (symbolized by Abel) are exterminated by the class of agriculturalists (symbolized by Cain). Soon new forms of institutionalized violence arise in great cities, so horrible that they are swept away by a flood of judgment. Eventually empires emerge, reflecting the imperial dream of unifying people under one dominating language and culture in Babel. Genesis provides a genealogy for all the pain and evil in the whole social structure of humans on planet Earth: it can be traced back to a problem of consumption beyond limits. [100]

By reading the rants of McLaren in the above quote, we can quickly see where interpreting the Scriptures with "relevance," "mythology" and "personal taste" will take us . . . man becomes god, a god that creates his own problems and then provides his own solutions.

NEWSFLASH! NOW HEAR THIS!: Origen, Aquinas, Nietzsche, Wellhausen, Derrida, Barth, Bultmann, Croatta, Gadamer, Alan Jones, Brian McLaren—*and his followers*—are ALL theological *deconstructionists*. STAY AWAY from these men and their teachings! [101]

Risking redundancy, I assert that *deconstructionism* is the chief cornerstone of the Emergent church!

---

[100]   See *www.extremetheology.com/2007/10/mclarens-new-bo.html* quoting Brian McLaren, *Everything Must Change—Jesus, Global Crises and the Revolution of Hope*, (Nashville, TN: Thomas Nelson, Inc., 2007), pg. 209-210

[101]   For more information, see Appendix #1

Deconstructionism allows and encourages total individual randomness among Christians to do what ever they please regarding the teachings of the New Testament. As a result, some pretty whacky stuff takes place! Wess Daniels adds this regarding some *deconstruction* variances;

> Many emerging churches have both men and women leaders and meet in houses, dance clubs, old warehouses or even bars. The main point is that for the emerging church old structures and ways of doing and being church are no longer valid for following Christ in a post modern world.[102]

We have had much to say regarding what the Emergents do NOT hold dear, but just what DO they hold dear? Previously cited denominationalist Dr. Gary Gilley contends that the "secret message of the kingdom," *i.e.* the purpose and the mission of the church, is NOT to save souls but to be "missional."[103] Being "missional" is one of the more dangerous concepts of *deconstructionism*. Open your eyes, you will see this word more and more on your bulletin boards, college lectureships and in brotherhood papers. We will

---

[102] Comments made by Wess Daniels on barclaypress.com in a review of the book; *Emerging Churches* by Ryan Bolger & Eddie Gibbs.

[103] Dr. Gary Gilley,—*op. cit.*

speak of this in a moment, just remember . . . when you hear the word "missional," think *"socialist action for the here and now."* "Missional" according to answers.com means;

> All believers are missionaries who are sent to be a blessing to the culture around them through a lifestyle that brings God's kingdom here on earth through verbal evangelism, social activism and however God has gifted the individual.[104]

Gilley puts it this way;

> ". . . missional" is; ". . . a kingdom focused on injustice, poverty, education, integrity, the environment, hospitality, medical care, the healing of the earth, pollution, exploitation, greed, etc." [105]

The most chilling definition of "missional" comes from the aforementioned neo-Gnostic apologist, Brian McLaren:

---

[104]   From answers.com/topic/emerging-church

[105]   Dr. Gary Gilley, - *op. cit.*

But my mission isn't to figure out who is already blessed [saved-RM], or not blessed, or un-blessable. My calling is to be blessed so I can bless everyone. I'm going to Los Angeles! [In lieu of heaven—RM]

Recently I received an e-mail saying, "I heard a rumor that you're a universalist. Is that true?" Since I don't offer my exclusivist [those who believe that some people will go to heaven but most will not-RM] friends their expected answer to "the hell question," I can see why this rumor would spread. Rumors like this make me want to be an exclusivist who believes that only universalists go to heaven—after all, they have the highest opinion possible about the efficacy and scope of the saving work of Jesus! Or else I could be an inclusivist [universalist—RM] who believes that all but exclusivists are going to heaven. But no, that's ridiculous. Anyway, I'm going to Los Angeles. The old universalism pronounces that the Good News was efficacious for all individual sold *AFTER* [emphasis Brian McLaren] death, in heaven, beyond history. Inclusivism says the gospel is efficacious for many, and exclusivists say for a comparative few. But I'm more interested in a gospel that is universally efficacious for the whole earth BEFORE (emphasis Brian McLaren) death in history. [106]

Now hear this: Brian McLaren does not believe in a literal heaven and hell where the obedient are saved and the disobedient are damned. He rejects the fact that the Scriptures contain the linearly clear, totally inerrant and 100% inspired Word of God! Brian McLaren believes in the "here and now" and could not care less about the "here after." Now hear this as well: Brian McLaren and his cabal are injecting this error into the church of Christ and want to bring it to YOUR congregation! More later on how he is accomplishing this goal.

Now this all "appears" to be "new and different," but is it? Is the "new and exciting" really what it claims to be? No, not at all! The theology of the Emergent church is somewhere between 1800 and 1900 years old! In the decades following the deaths of the apostles there arose two distinct schools of biblical interpretation, the Alexandrian and the Antiochene.[107]

---

[106]   Brian McLaren, *A Generous Orthodoxy—Why I Am a...*, (Youth Specialties Books/ Zondervan, El Cajon, CA. and Grand Rapids, MI., 2004), pg. 113-114. [Emphasis mine unless otherwise noted—RM]

[107]   I owe a great deal to my understanding of this material in this section to Walter C. Kaiser, Haddon W. Robinson and Berkeley Mickelson. For more detail see:

John warned repeatedly in his epistles that the faithful must affirm that Christ came in the flesh for "many antichrists are already in the world" denying the fact of His incarnation. The two schools arose on both sides of this volatile issue. The Alexandrian school, which by the way was open to anyone who wanted to attend and which taught many subjects other than theology, stressed the divine nature of Christ and downplayed His humanity. As a result of the intermingling of Christians and pagans, the pagan philosophies of Platonism and Gnosticism soon diluted the theological teachings of the school. The Antiochene school, singularly focused on theology, and, while not denying the divinity of Christ, emphasized His humanity. We are reminded that "for every action there is an equal and opposite reaction." We should note that by the time that these schools rose to prominence, time had marched into the third century, as much removed from Pentecost as we are from the birth of George Washington! Much

Walter C. Kaiser, Toward an Exegetical Theology—Biblical Exegesis for Preaching and Teaching, (Grand Rapids, Michigan: Baker Books, 1981, 2006) Chapter 2: "The Definition and History of Exegesis"

Haddon H. Robinson, Biblical Preaching—The Development and Delivery of Expository Messages, (Grand Rapids, Michigan: Baker Academic, 1980, 2001) Chapter 1: "The Case for Expository Preaching"

A. Berkeley Mickelson, Interpreting the Bible, (Grand Rapids, Michigan: William B. Eerdmans Publishing Company, 1963, 1977) Chapters 1 & 2: "Source of the Interpreter's Principles" & "Lessons from the Past" error, as it were, had already flowed under the theological bridge. We should also note that our faith is in Christ and His Word and NOT on what any man, any institution or any method may say or do. Fifty years ago, all of our Christian colleges taught the "whole counsel of God." We cannot say that today. We cannot put our faith in any school. We can put our faith only in God. The faith of many among the church of Christ is again being threatened by "dead men still speaking."

9. ORIGEN, A MAN THOUGH DEAD, STILL SPEAKS

As just noted, the Alexandrian school was favored by those influenced by Gnosticism and Platonic philosophy, most notably Origen preceded by his mentor, Clement. The more faithful church favored the Antiochene school whose most notable man was Lucian. The Alexandrians were more intellectual and wrote prolifically. The Antiochenes were more "hands to the plow" people and the church of Christ at Antioch had been heavily involved in mission work for literally hundreds of years, having first launched Paul and Barnabas in Acts 13. There were huge and distinct differences between the two schools. Origen and his allegorical interpretive approach dominated the Roman church from very early on and still does today. In April, 2007, the then sitting pope, Benedict XVI, reaffirmed the fact that Origen's allegorical (fictional stories with hidden meanings) interpretive method made possible the elevation of church tradition to equality with Scripture itself!

In our meditations on the great figures of the ancient Church, today we will get to know one of the most outstanding. Origen of Alexandria is one of the key people

116

for the development of Christian thought. *He draws on the teachings he inherited from Clement of Alexandria*, whom we reflected upon last Wednesday, and brings them forward in a totally innovative way, *creating an irreversible turn in Christian thought.* He was a true teacher; this is how his students nostalgically remembered him: not only as a brilliant theologian, but as an exemplary witness of the doctrine he taught. In substance, he grounded theology in the explanations of the Scriptures; or we could also say that his theology is the perfect symbiosis between theology and exegesis. In truth, the characterizing mark of Origen's doctrine seems to reside in his incessant invitation to pass from the letter to the spirit of the Scriptures, to progress in the knowledge of God. And this "allegoristic" approach, wrote von Balthasar, coincides precisely "with the development of Christian dogma carried out by the teachings of the doctors of the Church," who—in one way or another— accepted the "lesson" of Origen. In this way, Tradition and the Magisterium, foundation and guarantee of theological research, reach the point of being "Scripture in act."[108]

---

[108] Origene: il mondo, Cristo e la Chiesa," tr. it., Milano 1972, p. 43. (Benedict XVI. Homily On Origen of Alexandria. Vatican City. Zenit - April 25, 2007). [RM NOTE: According to the Catholic Encyclopedia On Line, *Magesterium & Tradition*

After the Muslims over ran Antioch in the seventh century, the by then apostate Roman church condemned as heresy pretty much everything and everyone associated with the Antiochene School. The linear interpretive approach of the Antiochene school melted into history until the Reformation as the Roman church continued it's freefall further into apostasy under the influence of Origen's allegorical interpretive model.

We cannot over emphasize the influence of Origen both then & now.

Origen's allegorical method led the Roman church into total doctrinal error and will do the same to our erring brethren if they do not turn away from subjective interpretive models, especially those taught by Alan Jones, Brian McLaren, Greg Taylor *et al,* as we will soon see.

Alexandrian (Alexandria, Egypt) theology did not just appear over night, it had quite an evolution. The Alexandrian School and allegorization of Scripture are synonymous terms, so synonymous

---

is defined thusly: *"The word refers sometimes to the thing (doctrine, account, or custom) transmitted from one generation to another sometimes to the organ or mode of the transmission."*]

as one cannot discuss one without the other. To do so would be like attempting to discuss Annapolis without the U. S. Navy! The ancient Greeks, influenced by Plato, interpreted the writings of Homer allegorically. ["Allegorical", is defined in *Webster's Ninth New Collegiate Dictionary* (1991) as, "having hidden spiritual meaning that transcends the literal sense of the sacred text." An allegory is defined as, "the expression by means of symbolic fictional figures and actions of truths or generalizations about human existence."] Plato taught that each physical reality has an unseen "spiritual" story behind it. Platonism allowed any group or individual to take any meaning they wanted from the Homeric text through the use of allegory. Why was the allegorical method so popular among the Greeks? There are two primary reasons. First of all, when a passage was seen as embarrassing allegory kept the presenter of the material from being laughed at "or even worse . . . ignored."[109] Secondly, wildly popular still today among the Emergents, allegory allowed the speaker or writer to use the writings of the past to promote CURRENT agendas! One could "twist" the meaning of a passage to suit his own pragmatic purposes. Mickelsen notes; "By allegorizing, Stoicism could show that it was at home with the past while at the

---

[109] A. Berkeley Mickelsen, <u>Interpreting the Bible</u>, (Grand Rapids, Michigan: William B. Erdmans, 1963, 1977) p. 28

same time it could bring a fresh message into its contemporary world."[110]

The Jews living in Hellenistic Alexandria found the allegorical method pragmatically attractive in "defending" Judaism. Things got so bad that about 150 B.C. an Alexandrian Jew by the name of Aristobulus actively taught that "Moses really taught Greek philosophy and that the Greek philosophers had borrowed their ideas from Moses."[111] Just prior to the Christian age, Philo aggressively promoted the allegorization of the Old Testament emanating his teachings throughout the dispersed Jewish world. His allegorical twist was similar to Thomas Aquinas' much later "reason over revelation" theory. It appears that Philo believed that the "literal meaning of the Scripture was LESS IMPORTANT than the "truth" revealed through Greek philosophy!" [112]

There is a salient point that must be made here: Origen could never have visualized, let along taught, allegorization of Scripture had it not been for the influence of Greek philosophy flowing through

---

[110]   Ibid. p. 28
[111]   Ibid. p. 28
[112]   Ibid. p. 29

Philo and Clement before him. Let's follow the clues through the forest!

An understanding of the theological landscape of Judea during the first third of the first century is greatly enhanced by a review of the popular interpretive methods of the time. Correct interpretation of the "law and the prophets" is central to the on-going dialogue between Jesus Christ and the religious leadership of the day. In fact, proper interpretation of the Old Testament is germane to the many theological confrontations Jesus had with the Pharisees, Sadducees, scribes and lawyers as recorded by the inspired authors of the four gospels. Jesus Christ, as the incarnate "Word of God" and one who came not to, abolish the law, but to "fulfill the law" fully, exposited the Old Testament clearly and boldly to the extent "that the people were astonished at His teaching . . . for He taught them as one having authority, and not as the scribes."—Matthew 7:28b-29 (NKJV)

Noting the enraged reaction from the religious establishment towards Jesus, we must ask ourselves the question, "What was it about Jesus' teaching that so angered and threatened the "elders of the people?" In addition to exposing their brazen hypocrisy, Jesus exposed the empty, erroneous and misguided interpretive models they were using to empower and enrich themselves at the expense of the people. God Incarnate brought the very same argument regarding the Word of God to the religious establishment of first century Judea that He had brought to King Saul through the prophet Samuel. The only difference was that with the 1st century Jewish leadership, Jesus did so in the flesh "eyeball to eyeball." We need to take heed, and take heed now, these urgent lessons taught to King Saul 30 centuries ago and to the Pharisees and the Sadducees 10 centuries later.

As it is crystal clear that the Jewish religious leadership of the early first century was in interpretive error, we must ask the question, "How did this come to be?" Ironically, the answer is the same as the question, "How did Roman Catholicism become apostate?" The answer to both questions is: TRADITION evolved first to *equality* to the Word of God and then to *superiority* to the Word of God. History is now repeating itself for "at least' the fourth time! Take note of these four moments in history when men decided that "tradition" trumps revelation:

1. First century Rabbinic tradition

2. Roman Catholic "tradition over revelation"

3. Reformational creeds in lieu of Scripture

4. The 21st century Emergent church movement

In the first century, the Jewish Scriptures were contained in just 3 collections. They were not separated out as is the Old Testament today. They were: 1) The Law, 2) The Prophets and 3) The "Writings." The Writings were the poetic and wisdom books. These were in written form BUT not publicly distributed outside the Temple and the various local synagogues. The vast majority of the population knew the Word of God by oral communication only. They heard the Word of God read every Sabbath day, memorized it and then taught it to their children by repetitive drills of various kinds as described in Deuteronomy 6:4-9.

Approximately 500 years before Christ, the faithful remnant began to collect oral commentary on the Law, the Prophets and the Writings. They were passed along from generation to generation in an attempt to replicate the work that Ezra did after the return of the people to Babylon when he had the Law read to the people as well as "giving the sense" in what we would call today the "expository manor." Unfortunately, in those 500 intervening years, the "oral tradition," now referred to as the "Halakah" or "Halachah," had evolved from commentarial status to orthodox status. No longer did the Rabbi's go the Word of God directly, they came to God's Word via the "Halakah," thus rendering it superior to Scripture. By Jesus' day, the "Halakah" had at best clouded the Word of God and at worst, supplanted it. So when we come to the gospels, the Word of God (Jesus Christ Incarnate—John 1) taught the "whole counsel of God" as doctrine, while his contemporaries taught the "traditions of men" as doctrine. (See Matthew 15:1-20 and Mark 7:1-23 as Jesus exegetes Isaiah 29:13-14) A more stark contrast could not be imagined. Revelation vs.Tradition. Where do you stand, dear reader? Kaiser observes the following regarding their *Targums* (explanations) of the Scriptures during the time of Christ:

. . . oral teaching became a fixed and growing supplement to the biblical text, gradually possessing an authority equal to that of the Scriptures. The claim was that this tradition was handed down faithfully from the scribe Ezra and the members of the Great Synagogue, who in turn were alleged to have received it by divine revelation. [113]

Kaiser observes further:

As the Christian era dawned, it was customary for the Jewish rabbis to distinguish between two senses of the text: the *peshat,* the "clear," "plain," or "simple" (hence the literal or historical) meaning of a Bible passage; and the *remaz,* the hidden sense of the Mosaic law and of the Halakah. There also was the *derush* ("searched") meaning of Scripture, that is, the allegorical sense expressed in the form of *hagga-doth,* or legends . . .

The exegesis dealing with historical and dogmatic subjects was called *haggadic midrash.* This type of interpretation was more illustrative, practical, and mixed with a wealth of allegory, legend and colorful biblical history. It was mainly a homiletic approach to the study of the Bible. In contrast, the exegesis dealing with legal matters was called *halakic midrash.* This form of interpretation attempted to apply

---

[113]   Walter C. Kaiser, Jr. and Moise's Silva, *op cit,* pg. 258.

the law, by analogy and by a combination of texts, to those exceptional cases for which there was no special enactment in Moses' law. [114]

By the first century, three main Jewish sects represented three interpretive variants regarding the Law and the Halakah while they jockeyed for dominance in the culture. They were: The Rabbi's, The Qumran Sect and the Jewish Diaspora. The Qumran Sect was small, secluded and without any influence, and, the Scriptures are silent regarding them. We will not, therefore, examine their minimal impact. The Rabbi's and The Diaspora (dispersion) battled it out "for the souls of men." The Rabbi's were more linear and less circular in their interpretive method. Their most notable man was Rabbi Hillel (30 B. C.—A.D. 15) who lived just before the time of Christ's ministry. The Rabbi's were, what we could call today, "traditional mainstream." They wanted to preserve Israel in the post-exilic reflection of Ezra and Nehemiah but did not segregate themselves from society like the Qumran Sect nor did they adopt "pragmatic Hellenism" like those of the Diaspora. The interpretive model of the Rabbi's was what this author would characterize as "linear w/ blinders." They interpreted the Law literally but far too much so.

---

[114]   Kaiser and Silva, *op cit,* pg. 258

They could not hear what Christ had to say, though Christ literally stood in their midst. They eventually joined their enemies in a united front to murder the Son of God. As we have stated elsewhere, just HOW we interpret the Bible does have consequences!

The need for proper interpretation of the Scriptures became acute when the Israelites returned to Jerusalem after spending 70 years of exile in pagan Babylon. While there, not only did they forget their native Hebrew language, they forgot the Word of God. After their return from exile, Ezra the priestly scribe reads the Law of Moses to the people and uses other priests to scripturally "give the sense" of the Word as well. Ezra was a "skilled scribe" in the Law of Moses according to Ezra 7:6.

In the years following Ezra's death, the remnant of God's people began gathering the oral teachings of the scribes who succeeded the great scribe. Little by little, these oral teachings (the Halakah) were preserved and eventually became part of what later became known as the *Talmud.* Kaiser explains:

> Some parts of the *Talmud* can be traced back to the second
> century B. C., when various teachings began to be handed

down orally and constantly augmented in each generation. Then, in the second century A. D., Judah Ha-Nasi collected these teachings in written form. This work, which consists of sixty-three tractates, became known as the *Mishnah*. In the course of time, the *Mishnah* itself was the subject of a written interpretation, the *Gemara*. The combination of the *Mishnah* and the *Gemara* is generally referred to as the *Talmud*. [115]

At the end of the day, the Rabbis, despite their good intentions and despite their "relative" conservatism, fell into the same interpretive trap as did their theological counterparts—they lifted their traditions to the level of orthodoxy. This false orthodoxy built upon layers of oral tradition was what Jesus Christ came to face from the most "faithful" among the remnant. We know these men by their more common name—Pharisees.

The Pharisaical counterpart was the Sadducee. Though we speak of this very little today, the Diaspora had an extreme influence

---

[115]   Kaiser and Silva, *op cit,* Footnote #3, pg. 259. NOTE: It is upon these allegorical and subjective commentaries that modern day Judaism is built. That is why today's Judaism has little to no commonality with the Law of Moses as revealed in the Old Testament.

on the Jewish culture of the 1st century. The Diaspora (dominated primarily by the Sadducees) was more circular and less linear in their interpretive method. During the domination of Judea by the Greeks, many Jews fled Israel and were "dispersed" throughout the known world. The intellectual center of the Diaspora was Alexandria, Egypt. The Septuagint translation of the Hebrew Scriptures into Greek were penned in Alexandria by "The 70" (LXX). Unfortunately, as we discuss elsewhere, Alexandria was the center of the "allegorical" universe. The most educated and powerful Jews in the world were from Alexandria and managed to exert tremendous influence back in the "old country." The Diaspora represented the "higher criticism school," as it were, of Judaic religious tradition. As we know from Scripture, the Sadducees did not believe in the resurrection nor the existence of angels. It is likely that they rejected the existence of the soul itself. The Diaspora, by and large, and their Sadducee disciples, were skeptics, barely believing in God at all. They did not respect the integrity of God's Word, embracing instead the foolishness of allegory. They rejected the very notion of useable hermeneutics, leaving their adherents to grope in the dark looking for truth but never finding it. Both the Diaspora and the Sadducees were apparently heavily influenced by Hellenistic polytheism, the self dependency of Stoicism and the self indulgence of Epicureanism. [116] The Greek culture tail wagged the Jewish theological dog.

The most influential man among the Alexandrian Diaspora was Philo (ca. 20 B. C.—A.D. 50). Remember Philo. His allegorical interpretive methods greatly influenced Clement who, in turn, greatly influenced Origen, "a man though dead still speaks." [Brian McLaren's theology replicates Philo, Clement and especially Origen.] Kaiser observes the following regarding Philo and the Alexandrian method of interpretation:

> Much of the inspiration for the Hellenistic scholarship [at Alexandria—RM] was derived from the concept that the Scriptures bore a deeper truth, or spiritual sense, called the *hyponoia.* This deeper truth lay under the human words and had to be uncovered by means of allegorical interpretation. This allowed the text to say something other than what the words meant. [117]

---

[116] See: http://en.wikipedia.org/wiki/Sadducees - "History," paragraph #1

[117] Kaiser & Silva, *op. cit.* pg. 261

How did this line of thinking play out in "real life" for Philo? Kaiser answers:

> Whenever Philo was confronted with what he perceived were impossibilities, impieties, or absurdities in the biblical text, he carefully searched for clues, such as mysterious numbers, etymologies, peculiar expressions, or the like that could unravel the real teaching of the *hyponoia* behind the surface meaning. [118]

We have labored long on this point but we must realize that there indeed is "nothing new under the sun." Today's Brian McLaren was yesterday's Plato, Philo, Clement, Origen amd Aquinas. As went Alexandria so went Jerusalem. Ironically, the Sadducees fell into the same trap as did their theological adversaries, the Pharisees—they elevated their philosophical assumptions to the level of orthodoxy placing themselves, along with the Pharisees, on a collision course with the Creator of the universe!

Were that the false notions of the Rabbi's and the Diaspora died in 70 A. D. with the Jewish national state! Unfortunately, allegorical error

---

[118] Kaiser & Silva, *op. cit.* pg. 261-262

like cancer, spread into the church of Christ even before the deaths of the apostles from Hellenistic influenced Jews. Our brothers Peter, John and Jude actively engaged protognostic heresy in their inspired epistles. Brother Paul clearly warned of the soon coming apostasy that would arise from the ranks of extant elderships (Acts 20:25-31) and foretold of doctrinal variances soon to come (I Timothy 4:1-5).

Platonic thinking and interpretive models influenced many in the early years of the church, including first Clement of Alexandria who then influenced Origen, the most influential Patristic when it comes to biblical interpretation. Mickelsen has the best working definition of the allegorical method I have found:

> In the allegorical method a text is interpreted apart from its grammatical historical meaning. What the original writer is trying to say is ignored. What the interpreter wants to say becomes the only important factor. [119]

Lampe & Woolcombe have a salient observation regarding the allegorical method as well; ". . . . allergorism is the search for secondary and hidden meaning underlying the primary and obvious

---

[119] Mickelson, *op. cit.*, p. 28 [Emphasis mine RM]

meanings of a narrative." [120] They cite an example from a sermon delivered by the Patristic Chrysostom who *brutally* allergorizes Matthew 2:16-18:

> The fact that only the children of two years old and under were murdered while those of three presumably escaped is meant to teach us that those who hold the Trinitarian faith will be saved whereas Binitarians and Unitarians will undoubtedly perish. [121]

Mickelsen then summarizes the allegorical method:

> The allergorist takes any narrative (even though the original author gives no indication of having his assertions stand for something else) and after ignoring the primary or obvious meaning, he arbitrarily attaches to the narrative the meaning he wants to convey. In practice he treats the narrative in such a way as almost to deny its historicity . . ."[122]

---

[120] Mickelsen, *op. cit.,* p. 238 quoting: G. W. H. Lampe and J. J. Woolcombe, <u>Essays on Typology</u>, Studies in Theology Series, (London: SCM Press, 1957) p. 39

[121] Ibid. p. 238 - 239 quoting: G. W. H. Lampe and J. J. Woolcombe Ibid. p. 31 -32

[122] Ibid. 238

Origen's interpretive system assessed nearly the entire body of scripture allegorically, though proportionately precious little of the Bible is written in an allegorical style. In fact, there is only ONE passage that is said to be an allegory! The word "allegory" appears only in Galatians 4:21-24:

> Tell me, you who want to be under law, do you not listen to the law? For it is written that Abraham had two sons, one by the bondswoman and one by the free woman. But the son of the bondswoman was born according to the flesh, and son of the free woman through the promise. This is *allegorically* speaking, for these women are two covenants: one proceeding from Mt. Sinai bearing children who are to be slaves; she is Hagar.—(NASB)

It is interesting that Paul's "allegory" doesn't remain one but an instant! Why? Because the HIDDEN message inherently imbedded in any allegory is REVEALED instantly by Paul! Origen obsessed in the "hidden message" of allegory while Paul rushes to interpret the only real allegory in the New Testament! Had Paul NOT revealed the hidden meaning of the allegory by inspiration of the Holy Spirit, this quotation would have indeed remained as allegory.

This revelation means that Paul's "allegory" is NOT allegorical, it has instead become metaphorical for God's revelation has removed ALL speculation as to what the passage means. It bears repeating, an allegory is a fictional illustration of a fictional statement whereby the reader can assign his multiple and individual meanings. A metaphor, on the other hand is a factual illustration of already established truth. Revelation is rock solid and unquestionable TRUTH. Unfortunately, Origen would have us thinking, along with the rest of the Scriptures, that this passage remains an allegory. It does not. Much and grievous error has arisen, and continues to arise, because of bro. Origen's allegorical error. Humans relish "searching for truth" but are in terror of actually finding it. Once found, truth demands responsibility before God because of sin. "IF" people can stay in the never ending circular "search" for truth, lives never change. Jesus said; "Unless you repent, you shall all die in your sins." Conviction of sin is never found in the allegorization of the Scriptures as the method is inherently self deceptive and self centered. Allegrization means that a person can force his or her "views" upon the Word of God, thus becoming a "god" himself sitting, as it were, in judgment upon the words spoken by the Almighty. Pretty scary for a "jar of clay" to assume such power!

In conclusion, denominationalist John MacArthur observes this regarding this passage:

> All allegory is a fictional story where real truth is the secret, mysterious, hidden meaning. The story of Abraham, Sarah, Hagar, Ishmael and Isaac is actually history and has no secret or hidden meaning. Paul uses it only as an illustration to support his contrast between law and grace. [123]

Though having no evidence to support his allegorization of Scripture, Origen persisted. Philip Schaff, the preeminent 19th century historian says this regarding Origen:

> His leaning to idealism, his predilection for Plato, and his noble effort to reconcile Christianity with reason, commend it even to educated heathens and Gnostics, led him into many grand and fascinating errors. [124]

---

[123] John MacArthur, The MacArthur Study Bible, (Thomas Nelson, Inc., Nashville, Tennessee, 2006), Study Notes, pg. 1765

[124] Phillip Schaff, History of the Christian Church Vol. II, (New York, New York: Charles Scribner's Sons, 1883(?), 1910) p. 371

Origen was born ca. 185 and led a very vigorous existence. The sheer amount of writing he did in his life is enough to boggle the mind, even at today's standards. In regards to biblical interpretation he honored 3 basic concepts. Later he added the fourth. His methods were layered. Here they are:

1. *Grammatical/Historical*—Correctly, he found that discovering the original grammar and history of a passage was essential.

2. *Moral*—Each Scripture contains a moral teaching.

3. *Pneumatic*—Each Scripture has a "spiritual meaning," a special or hidden message to the reader from the Holy Spirit.

4. *Multiple Meanings*—When Origen got to #3, he had a problem. Since the pneumatic teachings of the Scripture were found "allegorically" and that different readers and hearers assigned different stories to understand the Scriptures, he came to the conclusion that there had to be MULTIPLE MEANINGS for most, if not all of God's word.

Here is what an internet profile on Origen concludes:

> On this method the sacred writings are regarded as an
> inexhaustible mine of philosophical and dogmatic wisdom;
> in reality the exegete reads his own ideas into any passage
> he chooses.[125]

Unfortunately when Origen's allegorical method is actually applied, #3 and #4 could "trump" #1 and #2. That is why in Roman Catholic theology, church tradition *i.e.*, church councils and *ex cathedra* statements from the pope "trump" Scripture. Oh, that bro. Origen could have seen the fruit of the seed he sowed! In a very sad way, Origen "being dead, still speaks."

We can look at the 3 Fold/4 Fold Allegorical Method that Origen put together and scratch our heads wondering, "Why did he turn to allegorization and where did he get the concept?" Unfortunately, as King Saul before him, Origen looked around and about and turned to pragmatic rationalism to "tweak" God's will for a "good cause." Origen's "good cause" was a "need" to "defend" the church in Alexandria. Alexandria was awash with Greek culture and was

---

[125]   From nndb.com/Origen

also the home of the largest Jewish population outside of Israel. Since Christianity was rooted in Judaism, the Greek philosophers had a hay day criticizing a number of historical records in the Old Testament that "seemed" embarrassing. Mickelsen lists a number of problematic (problematic to the "wisdom seeking" Greeks, that is) instances that "needed" "apologetic assistance." Among these were "Lot's incest, the drunkenness of Noah, Jacobs wives and concubines, Judah's seduction of Tamar, etc . . . ." [126] Origen turned to allegory to "explain" these instances to his Greek friends with "stories" instead of exegesis and exposition. In other words, instead of being accounts of revealed truth regarding real people, Origen taught them as stories with hidden meanings that "softened" the "rough edges" of what the Greeks otherwise would have rejected outright. Origen's motivation flowed from an out-come based goal of "reason over revelation" with conviction taking a back seat, a classic example of battling the enemy on the ground of his own choosing.

Origen, having made his choice based upon pragmatic conjecture, now searched for his "proof text." Where could he turn for the

---

[126]   Mickelsen, *op. cit.,* p. 32

theology that would back up the surrender of his conviction? He settled on I Thessalonians 5:23. [127]

> And now may the God of peace sanctify you wholly; and I pray God your whole *spirit* and *soul* and *body* be preserved blameless unto the coming of our Lord Jesus Christ." (KJV)

Here's how Origen laid out his "thesis."

- Body: Real, observable and fleshly events

- Soul: Intimacy and involvement with other people

- Spirit: God's communication with man and man's communication to God

Believing it to be overridingly important, Origen stressed the Spirit far more than he did body and soul. With his "license to interpret" now in place, he came up with some amazing and head scratching conclusions!

---

[127] Mickelsen, *op. cit.,* p. 32

According to him [Origen—RM] Rebecca's drawing water for Abraham's servant and his cattle means that we must come to the wells of Scripture in order to meet Christ. In the story of the triumphal entry the ass represents the letter of the Old Testament; the colt or foal of an ass (which was gentle and submissive) speaks of the New Testament. The two apostles who obtained the animals and brought them to Jesus are the moral and spiritual senses. [128]

Following Origen, others took up the mantle of allegorical methodology.

Jerome (*ca.* 347-419) early on tried to throw off the allegorical method but embraced it eagerly when he wrote about the 44 stations in the Sinai wilderness. To Jerome, EACH station had a hidden and allegorical meaning. Regarding Jerome, Farrar says; ". . . his "multiple senses" and "whole forests of spiritual meanings" are not worth one verse of the original." [129] Jerome in a letter to Pammchius freely admits his addiction to allegory:

---

[128] Mickelsen, *op. cit.,* p. 32

[129] Mickelsen, *op. cit.,* p. 34 quoting H. H. Farrar, "The Bible: It's Significance and Authority," <u>The Interpreter's Bible</u>, I, 5-7

I not only admit but proclaim when translating the Greek, with exception to the Bible, *I don't translate word-for-word but sense-for-sense.* But my critics should also realize that translating the Bible *one must consider the intent and not merely the literal words.*[130]

The Roman heresy has always been enamored with allegorical interpretive methods since Origen. Not only that, as we can see from the quote, there are two schools of thought in regards to Bible translation that still hold true today. One can choose a "word-for-word" translation such as the **English Standard Version** ® or a "sense-for-sense" translation such as the **New International Version** ®. One can depend upon the precise meaning of ancient words accurately translated OR one can depend on the "perceived intent" of an author nearly two thousand years dead. Only one of these two options is achievable in our day and time and that is the former. The latter leads to a "smoke and mirrors" theology where one allows the "noble ignorance" of our day to superimpose ones subjective conclusions upon the Sacred Text. When tempted to take Jerome's course one should take note of what the translator deals with—the

---

[130] POSTSCRIPT March 27, 2013: As quoted in **Passages,** a privately owned collection of manuscripts and ancient Bibles that was on display in Charlotte, NC during the 1st quarter of 2013. *Italics added for emphasis - RM*

very Word of God. There is a colophon (**Websters 1828** defines colophon as "The conclusion of a book, formerly containing the place or year, or both, of it's publication.") that has been discovered in a 16th century scriptorium (a facility where a plurality of scribes copied the Bible from older texts): "O reader, take note while the hand that copied this text rots in the grave the Word copied lives forever."[131]

Augustine (354-430) used allegory in formulating his own personal theological philosophy after Ambrose who had allergorized Paul's statement in II Corinthians 3:6. Paul states that "the law killeth but the spirit makes alive." By adopting allegory, Augustine could now ignore all the "brutality" of the Old Testament he had rejected as a young man by assigning stories to it and, therefore, explain it away. Here's how Augustine allegorized the Fall of Man as recorded in Genesis 3:

- Fig Leaves = Hypocrisy

- Covering of Skins = Morality

---

[131] Ibid.

- Four Rivers = Four Cardinal Virtues [132]

Augustine grew even bolder in his allegorization mindset:

> . . . for Augustine in the parable of the good Samaritan the injured man became Adam who was leaving the heavenly city (Jerusalem) headed for the moon (Jericho, standing for our morality) but was waylaid by the devil and his angels (robbers) that led him into sin (wounds). The priesthood and the ministry of the Old Testament (the priest and the Levite) refused to help, but Christ (the Samaritan) healed him (oil=comfort or compassion, wine=blood) and led him via the incarnation (donkey) to the church (the inn). The innkeeper is the apostle Paul and the two denarii's are the command to love or the promise of life now, and life to come. [133]

---

[132] Mickelsen, *op. cit.,* pg. 34 referencing Augustine, <u>Concerning Christian Doctrine</u>, Chpts. 24-28, 42

[133] Grant R. Osbore, *op cit,* pg. 308 quoting: Klyne Snodgrass, "From Allegorizing to Allegorizing: A History of the Interpretation of the Parables of Jesus," In <u>The Challenge of Jesus' Parables</u>, Ed. R. N. Longenecker, pp. 3-29, (Grand Rapids, MI, 2000), pg. 4

The above examples, I confess, are extreme by today's standards but they are illustrative of the how far the human mind can go when it disconnects the concept of absolute inerrancy from the Word of God. Though humorous to us today, these examples are a warning to us to avoid the far more devious and damning current day interpretive errors that are, unlike the well meaning Augustine, made by cynics, Darwinists, agnostics and existentialists. "Rise up o men of God!" must be our cry!

The theories of Origen did much damage to the church of Christ as did a man who followed him by about 900 years—Thomas Aquinas, "a man though dead still speaks."

10. Thomas Aquinas, a Man Though Dead, Still Speaks

Other than Origen, no one has more influence on 21st century allegorical (circular) interpretation than does Thomas Aquinas (1225-1274 a.d.) Onto the template of allegorization, he added a second layer, that of "reason over revelation." As with Origen, Aquinas took the "poison pill" of Greek philosophy and blended it with revelation which, as always, produced a crop of deadly error. Origen favored Plato while Aquinas favored Aristotle. Using Plato, Origen introduced "multiple meanings" and upon that sand based foundation, Aquinas used Aristotle to introduce the idea that man could come to know God outside of revelation via his own natural senses. Aristotle's philosophy is summed up thusly; "Nothing is in the intellect that is not first in the senses."[134] We need to realize that Aquinas ADDED to the fives senses the "power of understanding, *imagination* and memory." [135] When one defines "imagination" as TRUTH, we have an open door to any and every variance from truth possible.

---

[134] Aristotle, De Anima, 3.8 as quoted by Richard Bennett in "Alan Jone's Reimagining Christianity: The Way Back to Rome," p. 5, as published on www.bereanbeacon.org/AlanJones/pdf.

[135] Ibid. p. 6

When "Thomism" [the philosophical teachings of Thomas Aquinas] is taken to its natural conclusion, the Apostle Paul and the late John Lennon are peers, each with an equally valid point of view!

But what does the Word of God have to say about "imagination?" Is it favorable or not? According to **Strong's,** the word "imagination" appears fifteen times in the KJV. Fourteen out of fifteen times, the word is used detrimentally towards the Aquinas model. The only exception is found in I Chronicles 29:18 when the word translated "imagination" is used in the connotation of "conception of thought" [per **Strong's**] as opposed to the continual "evil musings" of fallen man. Of the remaining fourteen uses, twelve are in the Old Testament. The word translated "imagination" is most often (nine times) the Hebrew word *shriyruth*, which according to **Strong's** means, ". . . twisted, that is, firm; obstinacy, lust." Here is a review of the fourteen detrimental uses of "imagination" in the KJV:

- Genesis 6:5—Every *imagination* of the thoughts of his [man's] heart was only evil continually . . .

- Genesis 8:21— . . . the *imagination* of mans heart is evil from his youth . . .

147

- Deuteronomy 29:19-20— . . . Though I walk in the *imagination* of mine heart, to add drunkenness to thirst: the Lord will not spare him . . .

- Deuteronomy 31:21— . . . I know their *imagination* which they go about . . .

- Jeremiah 3:17— . . . All nations shall be gathered unto it [the throne of the Lord], to the name of the Lord, to Jerusalem: neither shall they walk any more after the *imagination* of their evil heart.

- Jeremiah 7:24—But they hearkened not, no inclined their ear, but walked in the counsels and in the *imagination* of their evil heart, and went backward, and not forward.

- Jeremiah 9:14—But [they] have walked after the *imagination* of their own heart, and after Baalim, which their fathers taught them.

- Jeremiah 11:8—Yet they obeyed not, nor inclined their ear, but walked every one in the *imagination* of their evil heart . . .

- Jeremiah 13:10—This evil people, which refuse to hear my words, which walk in the *imagination* of their heart, and walk after other gods to serve and to worship them . . .

- Jeremiah 16:12— . . . Ye have done worse than your fathers; for, behold, ye walk every one after the *imagination* of his evil heart . . .

- Jeremiah 18:12— . . . There is no hope: but we will walk after our own devises, and will every one do the *imagination* of his evil heart.

- Jeremiah 22:17—They say still unto them that despise Me, the Lord hath said, ye shall have peace; and they say unto every one that walketh after the *imagination* of his own heart, no evil shall come upon you.

- Luke 1:51—(From the discourse of Elizabeth)—He hath shewed strength with his arm; he hath scattered the proud in the *imagination* of their hearts.

- Romans 1:21—Because that, when they knew God, they glorified him not as God, neither were they thankful; but became vain in their *imagination*, and their foolish heart was darkened.

We can conclude, therefore, "IF" one were to build a theological "system" on "imagination," it would be—according to Scripture—a Satanic one. The Word of God is anything but flattering towards man's "imagination." As strange as it sounds, Aquinas saw "imagination" as one of the "senses" and, in his mind, a prominent vehicle of truth. As mentioned, Aquinas believed that truth is primarily delivered by the senses not by revelation. This is a very old and very Romanesque concept, one that was born in paganism.

In his ***Commentary on Peter Lombard's Sentences*** *(III, 9, 2, 3)*, Aquinas says that there are three reasons to introduce *images* [imagination—RM] in the church.

First, to give instruction to the ignorant, to recall the Mystery of Incarnation and examples of the saints by their everyday representation; to nourish feelings of devotion, *better excited by vision than by audition.* [136]

Aquinas' theories are totally subjective and extra-biblical. Along with Origen's "multiple meaning" approach to Scripture, Thomism's "imagination is truth" not only CHANGES the revealed Word of God, it REPLACES it! In Roman Catholic theology truth comes from revelation (Scripture), tradition [the combination of "imagined truth," historical church practices, the creedal conclusions of church councils along with the writings of the various recognized saints and more recently (late 19th century) *ex cathedra* statements from the pope. Truth to a Roman Catholic is like a three legged stool:

Scripture + Tradition + *ex cathedra* papal statements = Truth

Unfortunately, whenever there is a conflict (and there always is!) between Scripture, tradition and *ex cathedra* statements— tradition and *ex cathedra* statements ALWAYS trump Scripture.

---

[136] See www.arsdisputandi.org. Roger Pouivet, "Religious Imagination and Virtue Epistemology," page 2, (emphasis RM). Type in the title of the article on the "Search Page" to read the article.

Why so? Simply because Aquinas taught that human reason, including the "sense" of imagination is the PRIMARY road to truth and the Scripture, by default, is therefore SECONDARY. Even more damning, Aquinas taught, as noted in the Lombard quote above that the *visual* sense is superior to the *auditory* sense in the communication of truth. You've heard the saying, "seeing is believing?" That's classic Thomas Aquinas and it could not be more in error! The Scripture clearly speaks otherwise, "So then, *faith* cometh by *hearing* and hearing by *the Word of God.*"—Romans 10:17 (KJV, emphasis added—RM) "IF" "seeing is believing," why did not ALL the Jews who had just witnessed Jesus raising Lazarus from the dead believe? Why did the Jewish leadership want to kill BOTH Jesus and Lazarus?! (See John 11:1-12:11) Aquinas, in contrast, taught that "faith comes by sight and sight comes by images and imagination." Note the stark contrast between the two:

Paul: FAITH via HEARING via THE WORD OF GOD

Aquinas: FAITH via SIGHT via IMAGES & IMAGINATION

When the Roman church combined the teachings of Origen and Aquinas mystery replaced revelation, visual stimulation replaced knowledge and expressions of art replaced the preaching of the Word of God. Why did the Roman church adopt such a stand? Primarily they adopted this stand because they saw people as woefully ignorant, as Aquinas said they were, incapable of understanding the Word of God as it is written. [137] Secondarily they adopted this stand because the Roman church would become the sole owner and dispenser of truth . . . the kind of truth that could be manipulated and changed over time rendering ultimate power, wealth and honor to the pope and his underlings. Bro. Wayne Jackson makes this observation:

> . . . it must be recognized that Roman Catholic theology is subject to change at any time. Today's official dogma may be in tomorrow's theological trash can. In Romanism, "tradition" is to be valued equally with the Scriptures—even more so (Attwater 1961, 41-42). *Vox populi vox Dei* ("The voice of the people is the voice of God") is the mantra of this amalgamated system that has evolved by a blending of components from Judaism, Christianity and paganism (Ibid., 363-364). [138]

---

[137] Pouivet, *op. cit.*, pg. 2

[138] Wayne Jackson, "The "Pope" Ignites a Controversy," in the Christian Courier, July 17, 2007 quoting Donald Attwater, A Catholic Dictionary, (Macmillan, New York,

Why is this any cause of concern today in the churches of Christ? It is of alarming concern because the Emergent church has adopted "visual stimulation" and "expressions of art" as major teaching vehicles! They have adopted a "seeing is believing" theological approach. They have bought into the teachings of Thomas Aquinas "hook, line and sinker."

When one attends an Emergent church "worship" service and experiences dance, drama, story telling, canvas painting, poetry, etc., such a person is experiencing undiluted Thomism. Many have, and rightly so, decried these practices as catering to the "entertainment" appetites of 21st century church goers. Much more damning, however, is the fact that "visual stimulation" rejects the biblical mandate of "faith cometh by hearing and hearing by the Word of God!"

Lest you think me an alarmist, consider the following statement from the Kinetic Christian Church in Charlotte, N.C.:

It's our belief that churches worldwide have forgotten that at one time, the church was the place to go to see the arts

NY), 1961, pages 41-42 and 363-364

expressed as glory to God. Whether it was sculpture, music, stained glass, woodcarving or painting—the church had the corner on it. And the result was that people were drawn to God through the use of it. It is our intention to take back the arts for the glory of God. That is why you will see all the fine arts variously used in our services. [139]

I cannot emphasize this point more: Emergent theology among churches of Christ is essentially *Roman Catholic*. Emergent theology is *Roman Catholic* because it has the same identical foundation— Origen's "multiple meanings" and Aquinas' "reason over revelation" fueled primarily by the senses, one of which is the "sense" of "imagination," Pope Benedict XVI and Brian McLaren are on the same team . . . and . . . they would like to recruit you and me!

Today there are a number of proponents of the teachings of Thomas Aquinas. His views are known today by many as "natural theology." One notable scholar espousing "natural theology" is Alister E. McGrath, an Anglican form Oxford University in England. He mixes the views of Aquinas' and Origen in his book, ***Christianity's***

---

[139] See original "Kinetic Christian Church Launch Plan" at www.kineticchurch.com. (No longer available on-line.)

Dangerous Idea—the Protestant Revolution—a History from the Sixteenth Century to the Twenty-first [140] McGrath attempts to vigorously cast doubt on the idea that an individual can (or should (?) properly interpret the Bible. The evidence of God comes from human senses and reason [Aquinas] and what God says in revelation comes only in multiple meanings [Origen]. The result is a denominational mish mash of error where your interpretation is as good as mine so we wind up adopting a "can't we all just get along?" Rodney King pseudo kind of unity. McGrath, therefore, is a "conservative Brian McLaren" who is a "conservative Alan Jones," the agnostic and activist cleric who praises Aquinas profusely:

> Thomas Aquinas got up each morning, as it were, studied a pagan philosopher named Aristotle, and found his thought absolutely congenial and appropriate for creating and structuring Christian theology. Why was he never afraid of the conjunction? He was never afraid because truth from whatever source is from the Holy Spirit. [141]

---

[140] Alister E. McGrath, Christianity's Dangerous Idea - The Protestant Revolution - A History from the Sixteenth Century to the Twenty-first, (New York: HarperCollins, 2007)

[141] Alan Jones, Reimagining Christianity-Reconnect Your Spirit Without Disconnecting Your Mind (Hoboken, New Jersey: John Wiley and Sons 2005) p. 149

We will delve into the errors of Alan Jones a little later in more detail. Aquinas, had an exciting life including being kept prisoner by his own family for some fifteen months so that he would not become a monk! Seeing that he would not be deterred, he was allowed to enter the Dominican order in 1244. He was mentored by Albert the Great who introduced him to a project that had as its goal reconciling the pagan philosopher Aristotle to dark ages Christianity. Ever increasing interest in this pagan drove him to a singular study of his philosophy from 1268-1272 while serving as a theologian to the Papal Court in Italy. Origen's multiple meanings theory had led the apostate church into a love affair with the teachings of the so-called "church fathers," or more technically, the "Patristics." He compiled a commentary on the gospels called **Catena Aurea**, all based on the views of these men, many of whom espoused error. Having embraced "imagination" as foundational to "truth," Aquinas saw "visions" and believed that Christ spoke to him personally. It is reported that he believed that Jesus Christ actually spoke these words to him, "You have written well of me, Thomas, what reward will you receive?" Supposedly, Thomas replied, "None but yourself." [142] R. C. Sproul tells of another instance regarding Aquinas and his

---

[142] Everett Ferguson, *op. cit.*, pp. 485-490 referenced for historical facts contained in this paragraph.

"imaginary contacts" with biblical personalities. On November 26, 2008, during his daily radio program on Charlotte, NC radio station, WHVN, Sproul details an instance in the life of Aquinas. While writing commentary on a portion of Isaiah, Aquinas was in a quandary, not knowing the meaning of some unidentified passage. He went to bed without writing anything. In the middle of the night his scribe heard Aquinas talking in his room for about an hour. When the talking ceased, Aquinas called in the scribe and dictated a lengthy passage. Afterwards, Aquinas dismissed the scribe but the scribe refused to be dismissed until Aquinas told him with whom he was speaking earlier in his room. Making the scribe promise not to reveal the answer while Aquinas lived, he revealed to him that the apostles Peter and Paul "appeared" to him and explained the meaning of the Isaiaic passage. When bro. Rick Atchley says that the Holy Spirit "spoke" to him and "told him" to preach sermons espousing instrumental music in worship, he took a page right out of Thomas Aquinas' theology, a pseudo theology that is based upon imagination, delusion, conjecture and subjectivity. [143]

---

[143] Rick Atchley, *op. cit.,* "Both/And" Sermon #2, minute 5, second 30 marker. For complete quote, see Appendix #1, Section 2, "The "Both/And" Lessons Claim Extra-Biblical Latter Day Personal Revelation via The Holy Spirit Himself."

Not only did Aquinas pull "truth" out of thin air, he believed theological truth to be available both in and OUT of the Scriptures. "[Thomas] believed not only that there was all truth somewhere but also that there was some truth everywhere." [144] Such thinking is fine if you are studying biology, but not if your field is theology.

God reveals Himself theologically ONLY in Scripture and no where else.

So we see that Origen influenced Jerome, Augustine, and Aquinas. He continues to influence the adherents of Emergent theology today—even as we speak. "Test the spirits . . ." The fact of coming judgment is the "terror of the Lord" that motivates us to "persuade men!"—II Corinthians 5:11

In conclusion, Origen's allegorical method, later mixed with Aquinas' "imagination is truth" theory tattooed a paradigm onto biblical interpretation that went unchallenged for nearly a thousand years! Power hungry popes, dictatorial fiefdoms and amoral clerics found Origen's methods a weapon of "mass instruction" *par excellence*. The allegories were so favored by Rome that during

---

[144]   Everett Ferguson, *op. cit.*, p. 488

the dark ages the Bible actually disappeared outside of the Vatican and the local monasteries! Stories *about* God literally replaced the Word *of* God! Words mean things. The word *"story"* is certainly no exception.

The word *"story"* has, at its very core, a least a partial fictional premise. Such a premise should never be assigned to the Word of God. When we read about the Creation, the Flood, Noah, the Tower of Babel, Abraham, Moses, Jonah, Elijah, Elisha and Jesus Christ we are NOT reading "stories" we are reading the inerrant, clear, linear and revealed ACTUAL ACCOUNTS of real lives lived by real people in real time. The Bible contains NO EXAMPLES OF FICTION, save one, though metaphorical tools are often used. [145]

(Remember an "allegory" is a FICTIONAL illustration while a "metaphor" is a FACTUAL illustration. Allegorical "truth" is assigned by humans while metaphorical truth is REVEALED by God Himself in His Holy Word.) This is an essential concept we must grasp and grasp quickly. Romanism and the Emergent church

---

[145]   The one exception is found in the book of Judges 9:7-15 where Jotham tells the only true allegory in all of Scripture in an attempt to persuade the people of Shechem from making Abimelech king after the murder of his 70 brothers, sons of Jerub-Baal.

are enamored with "stories." So as not to appear juvenile, many Emergents now refer to "stories" as "narratives," a pragmatically more acceptable term. In other words, when you hear an Emergent preacher say "narrative," think "story." As mentioned before, the Emergent church likes to use words in new and different ways so as to SOUND biblical while BEING otherwise. The state motto of North Carolina, where I make my home, comes to mind. *Esse quam videri*—"To BE rather than to SEEM." We are called to BE faithful, rather than to SEEM faithful!

Peter Kreeft is a former Protestant turned Roman Catholic. He, like all adherents to Origen and Thomas Aquinas, is singularly focused on "stories." Noted below is a portion of an interview Peter Kreeft gave in 1996 to Ellen Haroutunian of *Mars Hill Review* that sheds much light on this error.

> MHR: You have state that you see some *mysteries* or truths better in concrete *stories* rather than in abstract concepts—in novels rather than philosophy. *How has that been true for you?*

PK*: It has been true for me* in my readings of C. S. Lewis, Chesterton, Tolkien, Charles Williams, Dorthy Sayers. These writers have plugged into the depths of the *Christian tradition.* Their *images and stories* have influenced me from below.

MHR: What do you mean by "below?"

PK: Let's use the *image* of water. A city is surrounded by walls and it is fighting a war. The enemy is trying to knock down the walls, but they can't do it because the walls are too strong. Then a great rainstorm comes. As the rain suddenly gets underneath the walls and softens the ground, the walls fall down and the city is conquered.

. . . Rational arguments are like bullets. They're useful, but if we're going to conqueror the city that is the world, we need rain and not just bullets. *Images and attractive symbols* are like the rain. They soften the ground as they seep into the *unconscious.* Lewis called it "baptizing the imagination."

MHR: Is the study of literature important for the church?

PK: It is crucial—absolutely crucial. We are still deeply influenced by *stories*. We learn morality more from *stories* than from anything else. If we're not good *storytellers*, and if we're not sensitive to good *storytellers,* we'll miss out on the most important means of enlightening ourselves and transforming our world apart from a living, personal example. [146]

Because of Aquinas' "imagination is a generator of truth" theory, Romanism has nearly discarded the Word of God as a source of truth. Though remaining as "a" source of truth, it is always trumped by tradition and *ex cathedra* papal statements, as mentioned previously. We see from Kreeft's comments that direct biblical revealed truth has little use for him. Unfortunately, the same can be said of the Emergent church. "Stories" and "images" are at the very heart of circular interpretation, the preferred method of both the Roman and the Emergent church as we shall soon see.

---

[146]   Ellen Haroutunian, "A Baptism of Imagination—A conversation with Peter Kreeft," Mars Hill Review 5 (Summer 1996): pgs. 56-73. (Emphasis added to denote Thomistic terms and concepts—RM)

Don't think for a minute that the Lord's church is somehow immune from "fictional" and "story book" influences. Post-Modern circular interpretive methods ask a never ending litany of questions while providing no answers. Bro. William Woodson quotes from *God's Holy Fire* [all three authors are members of the Lord's church] in a recent journal article:

> Today's readers may ask certain "modern" questions that may not help us arrive at the theological message of the text. We ask what really happened? Why do Egyptian records contain little or no mention of the plagues or the escape of the slaves? When did the exodus occur? Did natural phenomena (volcanic eruptions, red tides) cause the plagues? How many people left Egypt, millions or thousands? . . . All of these are legitimate questions for historians and scholars, Christians or not, come down in different places on them.

> But what is crucial for the church today is not the raw data of the history of the exodus and the subsequent events,

but the meaning of the story of the Exodus that Jews and Christians repeated over and over to their children. [147]

It is essential to garner the emphasis of the Emergent authors of this quote.

- First, they ASSUME that many "unanswerable" questions will be asked.

- Second they PRESUME to SUGGEST some such questions.

- Third they define their very own presumed questions to be LEGITIMATE.

- Fourth, they PREDICT that those answering these "questions" will "come down in DIFFERENT places on them."

---

[147]   Kenneth L. Cukrowski, Mark w. Hamilton, and James W. Thompson, God's Holy Fire (Abilene, TX: ACU Press 2002) pg. 99-100 *as quoted by* William Woodson, "The Danger of Modern Philosophy," The Spiritual Sword 39 (January 2008): pg. 15. [Emphasis added—RM] NOTE: Bro. Woodson is former chairman of the Bible Department at Freed-Hardeman University and retired Director of Graduate Studies in Bible at Lipscomb University.

- In conclusion they DISMISS all the questions and all the answers!

Finally they, as it were, throw up their hands in confusion and conclude that all that really matters is the "story."

A novice would have to conclude that "story" is an important, if not vital, biblical theme. Does the "story" have such a distinctive place in the Bible? Let's ask the Bible!

1. The word "story" is NOT mentioned in the New Testament.

2. The word "story" is mentioned twice in the Old Testament, both times in II Chronicles.

   a. II Chronicles 13:22—"And the rest of the acts of Abijah, and his ways, and his sayings, are written in the STORY of the prophet Iddo."

      1) The word "story" here refers to an entry in an extra biblical book no longer extant.

b. II Chronicles 24:27—"Now concerning his sons, and the greatness of the burdens laid upon him, and the repairing of the house of God, behold, they are written in the STORY of the book of the kings. And Amaziah his son reigned in his stead."

1) The word "story" here refers to an entry in an extra biblical book no longer extant.

3. The plural form of the word "story" is "stories." This word does not appear at all in the New Testament. It appears five times in the Old Testament, however, 100% of the time referring to the number of levels in a structure such as an ark or building.

The Emergent church, totally ignoring biblical precedent, makes a VERY BIG DEAL about "stories." In fact, the insignificant biblical "story" becomes the very CORNER STONE of their theology, replacing the ONE TRUE CORNER STONE, JESUS CHRIST! (Eph. 2:6; I Pet. 2:20)

The Bible IGNORES the term, COVER TO COVER, in the sense that Origen, Aquinas, the Roman Catholic Church and the Emergent church (both in and out of the churches of Christ) so long to use, or I should say MISUSE, the term. The Emergent church misuses the word "story" like the abortionists misuse the phrase "pro-choice."

The use of the word "story" or "stories" among us needs to CEASE when describing ANY biblical account! There is no such thing as a "Bible Story," a "Creation Story," a "Jesus Story" or a "RESSURECTION Story"! The very word "story" insinuates FICTION.

Luther grew up in an age of allegory, stories and theological fiction that is nearly beyond comprehension. I am told that Luther never even saw a Bible until he studied for his doctorate! There were two keys to the incredible success of the allegorical method. First of all, the congregants were *totally* illiterate. Secondly, the Roman clerics were *biblically* illiterate. *TODAY,* the Emergent church is enjoying great success because the congregants, though *able* to read and study, *choose* not to. Biblical illiteracy creates, if I may speak metaphorically, a "garage door" in the side of the church through which Satan drives a truck load of allegorical error. Alan Jones, Brian McLaren, *et. al.* are more than eager to open the door early and often.

Where does the allegorical method leave us? Mickelsen puts it well:

> Allergorizing is like a fog which at first renders objects indistinct and then finally blots them out altogether. In the presence of allergorizing both literal and figurative elements are obscured. [148]

The 1,300 year damage done by the allegorical method is nearly beyond description. The "Dark Ages" were dark because of a totally false interpretive method imposed upon the entire Western world by Rome. No one understood this more than Reformers Luther and Calvin. Opposition to Rome was not just an intellectual exercise in those years, it was life threatening. Listen to what the two Reformers have to say about the allegorical method:

Luther:

> Origen's allegories are not worth so much as dirt . . . allegories are empty speculations . . . the scum of Holy Scripture . . . allegories are awkward, absurd, invented, obsolete, loose rags . . . to use such a method for interpreting

---

[148] Mickelsen, *op. cit.,* p. 37

the Bible (would be to) denigrate . . . into a mere monkey game . . . allegory is a sort of beautiful harlot, who proves herself specially seductive to idle men. [149]

Calvin:

> It is an audacity akin to sacrilege to use the Scripture at our pleasure, and to play with them as with a tennis ball, which many before have done . . . it is the very first business of an interpreter to let his author say what he does say, instead of attributing to him what we think he ought to say. [150]

Were that we only had to deal with Origen and Aquinas! Several hundred years later we are spinning ever faster riding the circles drawn by these two misguided souls with the help of cynics, Darwinists, skeptics and agnostics

---

[149] Kaiser & Silva, *op cit,* pg. 270, quoting: Martin Luther, Lectures on Genesis, in Luther's Works, vols. 1-3, ed. Jaroslav Pelikan (St. Louis, MO: Concordia, 1958-61), comments on Gen. 3:15-20.

[150] Kaiser & Silva, *op cit,* pg. 270 quoting: John Calvin in his introduction to his Commentary on Romans.

11. Circular Interpretation And The "Fuller Sense"

Fast forward some 6 centuries past Aquinas to the "higher criticism" theology of the mid to late 1900's. With due respect, the people of Origen's time and up until the beginning of the "Age of Reason," people in the West understood that all truth was revealed by God Himself. Many, however, by the 19th century rejected divine inspiration. Only ever dwindling parts of the Scripture were actually inspired, according to many of that time. When these "biblical technicians" began to "interpret" the Scriptures, they chose a modified Origenian model. Denying the truth of the Gospel, Origen's multiple meaning theory was very attractive. Combine that with Aquinas' "reason over revelation" theory, we have a volatile potion of error. When all vestiges of revealed truth were removed what was left was something known as Circular Interpretation. Here's a technical definition:

Bible interpretation (hermeneutics) is therefore the *circular* (emphasis mine RM) process of understanding sacred Biblical literature, namely interpreting the component parts of the sacred text in the light of the whole and the whole of the light of its parts. It is the ongoing dialogue between one's initial understanding of the sacred text and the impressions of the Holy Spirit gathered from subsequent readings and reflections on it. It's the dialogue between one's own frame of reference (one's own sphere of existence) and the context of the text.[151]

Here is the working Circular Theology formula:

Origen + Aquinas—Revealed Truth = Circular Theology

Circular theology was a product, as just mentioned, of the "Age of Reason," where men arrogantly proclaimed that truth was primarily found through human reason. Now, during the Post-Modern age Circular Theology is even more bizarre for NOW, truth "cannot even be found" by human reason! Today's Circular Interpretation proclaims that the original meaning of the author is not knowable or important, that truth is discoverable inwardly and that truth is held individually. The best way to define today's circular theology is this: scripture has multiple meanings, each meaning is equally

---

[151] Ferdinand Deist, <u>A Concise Dictionary of Theological and Related Terms</u> (Pretoria, South Africa: Van Schaik, 1990, 1992)

valid and therefore when interpreting any given passage one ends where one begins; many questions and no answers. When circular theologians (either Platonic influenced Christians in the 2nd and 3rd centuries or Emergents in the 21st) sit around and discuss a passage, the conversation goes like this; "Well, this passage could mean thus or so OR it could mean the opposite OR it could mean something in between OR it could mean something we haven't even thought of yet." When the discussion ends, everyone leaves feeling good that they searched for the elusive "truth" and that each person in the discussion now owns their own equally valid and privately held "interpretation." Circular Theology promises no real answers, just real questions. After attending a Brian McLaren lecture at the 2004 ZOE Conference in Nashville, an attendee by the name of Tim Castle said this:

The best part of the day has been hearing McLaren speak. He reaffirmed some things I think I knew intuitively, but haven't been able to articulate. *He didn't give me the answers, but he's given me better questions.* [152]

[152] See http://timcastle.blogspot.com, September 30, 2004, "ZOE Conference Day," (emphasis added—RM)

Translating from "Emergent" back into English:

> "McLaren reaffirmed some things I think I imagined but just
> could find the words to describe. He had no answers but my
> questions now seem more intelligent!" This kind of silliness
> is not new, we saw it early in the twentieth century from
> the agnostic educator, John Dewey: "Although I have raised
> large questions, it is not my ambition to answer them." [153]

At the end of the day, there are no moral or religious absolutes and
one ends up like the people of Israel at the conclusion of the Period
of the Judges where; ". . . each man did what was right in his own
eyes." Here's what Barry Fuller of Fuller Theological Seminary says
in defense of the ambiguities of "circular theology;"

> Christianity's love affair with modernity and its
> universalizing tendencies created a climate in which the
> general assumption has been that what constitutes Christian
> faith has been "settled," and therefore any challenge to the
> status quo is often rejected as unbiblical or unorthodox.

---

[153] Dave Breese, *op cit,* pg. 161 quoting: Joseph Ratner, John Dewey's Philosophy (New York: Modern Library, 1938), pp. 245-246

The assumption is a singular understanding of the faith. [emphasis mine—RM] The easiest way to undermine different perspectives on issues like faith and practice during my lifetime has been to call someone's commitment to orthodoxy into question. But Christian faith is open to discussion. Historically it always has been. It can be questioned and reinterpreted. In fact, I would argue that it is meant to be questioned and reinterpreted. Religion is always a cultural production, and socio-cultural issues cannot be discounted from the ways in which we envision and understand faith. Issues and questions raised by our particular cultural situation not only inform but shape the various ways in which we interpret the gospel. If there ever was a time to question the status quo, it is now.[154]

Let's break down the theological components of the statement:

- He assumes that Christianity is "modern." It is not.

- He assaults the idea that the faith has been "settled." It has.

---

[154]   From Barry Fuller in <u>Christianity Today</u>'s blog; "Out of Ur." March 29, 2007. blog. christianitytoday.com/outofur/archives/2007/03/goodbye_religio_1.html

- He assaults the idea of singular interpretation.

- He assaults the idea of pointing out error as "judgmental."

- He asserts that the Bible can be and should be continually questioned and re-interpreted.

- He asserts that religion comes from culture, not revelation.

- He advocates an aggressive assault upon the status quo.

Circular Interpretation allows the adherent to literally turn the Word of God 180 degrees around on its head. The opposite of truth is error. Post-Modern Circular Interpretation is alive and well in the Emergent church movement and especially in the writings of Brian McLaren. In fact, perhaps nothing illustrates "circular interpretation" more than the name of McLaren's most widely read manifesto;

A Generous Orthodoxy—WHY I AM A missional + evangelical + post/protestant + liberal/conservative + mystical/poetic + biblical + charismatic/contemplative

+ fundamentalist/Calvinist + Anabaptist/Anglican + Methodist + catholic + green + incarnational + depressed-yet-hopeful + emergent + unfinished CHRISTIAN.[155]

After reading that, I feel like I just stepped off of one of those centrifugal force training machines they used to use to train Apollo moon shot astronauts! Whoosh! Whoosh! Whoosh!

The twin sister of the Alexandrian school "circular interpretation" is an interpretive method known as *sensus plenior,* the "fuller sense." Kaiser observes:

> This theory of *sensus plenior* would make the inspired writer a secondary element in the process and even a nuisance at times while God, the principal author, is viewed as supplying directly to interpreters many additional meanings that exceed those originally intended by the human authors. According to this view, though the same words are being investigated, normal rules of exegesis fail to yield as high a payload as when the exegete digs into the "fuller sense!"[156]

---

[155] Brian McLaren, *op. cit.*

[156] Walter C. Kaiser, Jr. Toward An Exegetical Theology - Biblical Exegesis for Preaching and Teaching (Grand Rapids, Michigan: Baker Books 1981, Seventh

A denominationalist by the name of Paul Achtemeier is quoted thusly regarding this subject:

> Paul Achtemeir (says) that not only are the original events inspired but also the meanings added by later communities are likewise inspired (1980). *Moreover, he affirms, we ourselves are inspired as we read it today.* [157]

The theory of *sensus plenior* was born years before Christ. It first appeared about 170 b.c. The rabbis ". . . instead of [using] their ingenuity to clarify the precise meaning conveyed by the language, they looked for "deeper hidden meanings."[158] During this time there was a rabbi by the name of Aqiba. He believed that every scripture held multiple hidden meanings. In fact it was said of Aquiba:

> He not only explained every particle and copula, but said that there was a mystic meaning in every letter of Scripture, and in every horn and letter flourish of every letter, "just as in every fiber of an ant's foot or a gnat's wing." The Rabbi's

---

Printing 2006) pgs. 109-110

[157] Grant R. Osborne, op. cit. pg. 25 NOTE: This is the philosophical error that led Bro. Rick Atchley to announce in December, 2006 that the Holy Spirit had spoken to him directly...or so it appears to this writer. [Emphasis added—RM]

[158] Mickelsen, *op. cit.,* p. 23

delighted to tell how "many rules unknown to Moses were declared by Aqiba." [159]

This philosophy assumes that end-users receive a message from God's Word that goes beyond the mindset and intent of the original author. In the end it arrogantly supposes that the Holy Spirit gives understanding to *people living today* that somehow goes beyond the understanding of ALL persons living in previous times, including the authors themselves! Like a "dynamic equivalent" Bible translation, the focus is on the audience and not on the author. What a person *hears* becomes more important than what God *says*. In order for this "logic" to work, the circular/Alexandrian/Origenian/ "multiple meaning" model must be promoted and the linear/ Antiochene/"singular meaning" model must be discarded. As in Paul Simon's song *The Boxer* ©, "Still a man hears what he wants to hear and disregards the rest."[160]

It is said that Augustine put it thusly; "If you believe what you like in the gospel, and reject what you don't like, it is not the gospel you believe, but yourself." [161] (Too bad he did not apply that same

[159]   Mickelsen, *op. cit.* pg. 26

[160]   Lyrics via lyricsfreak.com

[161]   Quote source: http://quotationbook.com/quote/4030/

principle to Romanism, transubstantiation and the allergorization interpretation of Scripture!) Again, we have come full circle back to the last verse in Judges.

When one adopts circular/Alexandrian/Origenian/multiple meaning /*sensus plenior* and Thomistic interpretive methods, it is easy to understand how "singing and making melody" morphs into rock and roll, Sunday suddenly becomes Saturday, the blood bought church of Christ turns out to be just another denomination and the Holy Word of God becomes just another story book.

12. THE SILENCE OF THE SCRITURES— ACCELERATOR TO LICENSE OR BRAKE ON PRESUMPTION?

How has this threat to the truth, just described, played out among churches of Christ? We have studied interpretive methods for years around the question, "Does the Silence of the Scripture allow us to go beyond what is written when living, serving and worshiping God?" The question has been centered on the use of the instrument in worship.

Until recent years we often studied Restoration History with the question; "How did the Lord's church divide over the use of the instrument?" In 1906, churches of Christ and the self-identified Christian Church were noted separately in the United States Census for the very first time. At the very core of that debate, then and now, is the question; "Does the silence of the Scripture give a green light to proceed beyond what is written?"

Those embracing a narcissistic view of history might claim that this question is one for our time exclusively. one that centers uniquely on the use of the instrument in worship and one that takes place only among "Restoration" churches. *They would be very wrong for assuming such.*

This issue is essentially the same issue that divided Samuel from Saul in I Samuel 15, the same issue that divided Remnant Judaism from Hellenistic Judaism, the same issue that divided Our Lord Jesus Christ from the Pharisees & Sadducees, the same issue that divided the inspired apostle John from the protognostics, the same issue that divided Alexandria from Antioch, the same issue that divided Rome from Germany, the same issue that divided the Zwingli Reformers from the Luther Reformers, the same issue that divided the church of Christ from the Christian church and now . . . the same issue that divides the church of Christ from the Emergent church!

> Luther was desirous of retaining in the Church all that was not expressly contradicted by Scripture, while Zwingle [original spelling in the primary text—RM] was intent on abolishing all that could not be proved by Scripture. The German Reformer wished to remain united to the Church of all preceding ages, and sought to purify it from everything that was repugnant to the word of God. The Reformer of

Zurich passed over every intervening age till he reached the times of the apostles, and, subjecting the Church to an entire transformation, laboured [original spelling in the primary text—RM] to restore it to its primitive condition. [162]

Those who departed from the truth in the late 19th century over the instrument adopted the "accelerator" side of the coin as did King Saul, Philo, the Pharisees & Sadducees, Origen, Aquinas, Pope Leo X and finally Luther himself! Where did this lead? It led to the conclusion by those who departed that anything not specifically disallowed in the Scripture was considered a *de facto* approval by God for ongoing faith and practice. Since there are no "thou shalt not" statements regarding the instrument, the departing instrumental faction declared their position "scriptural" as did King Saul *et al.* Today's advocates of the instrument should look around at the company they are keeping and in whose steps they are treading.

Unfortunately, this philosophy of change led to even greater error. We know that the radical wing of the Christian Church,

---

[162]   Jean Henri Merle D'Aubigne, <u>History of the Great Reformation of the 16th Century</u>, pg. 297 as referenced by Hugh Fulford, "The Protestant Reformation," Journal article in <u>The Spiritual Sword</u> "A Handy Guide to Church History," Vol. 39: July 2008: No. 4. pg 30. quoting D'AubIgne via Homer Hailey, <u>Attitudes and Consequences in the Restoration Movement</u>, (Roseemead, CA.: The Old Paths Book Club, 1952).

known today as the Disciples of Christ, has proudly claimed denominational status for decades. Their view of the silence of the Scriptures led them to adopt during the 1950's a concept known as "open membership." Essentially this doctrine says that if any person comes to a Disciple church claiming to be a Christian, who can say they are not? This very circular interpretation effectively did away with the essentiality of baptism for the remission of sins among the Disciples of Christ. Today, the Disciples of Christ are closer to Unitarianism than they are to the truth of the Bible. THAT is where the accelerator theory led THEM.

Lest we think that the more conservative in the instrumental faction were not as much affected I beg to differ. In 1971 I was a student at Oklahoma Christian College in Oklahoma City. Down the road several miles was a small college, Midwest Christian College now defunct and merged with Ozark Christian College[163] of Joplin, MO., run by the so-called "Independent Christian Church" a.k.a. the "Conservative Christian Church." One Christmas Eve one of my college professors visited their library to do some Restoration Movement history research. During his visit, a number of the people

---

[163]   See www.occ.edu

there on campus decided to hold communion in honor of the day. Christmas Eve that year was on a Saturday.

Their circular interpretation led them to hold communion on a day *unauthorized* in the New Testament in order to honor a day *unknown* and a day *uncelebrated* during the days of the apostles!

Unfortunately, we now know that a number of people from Ozark Christian College spoke at the 2008 Tulsa Soul Winners Workshop and brought their circular views with them.[164]

Circular Interpretation Is Coming SOON to a Congregation Near You via the Tulsa Workshop!

When one adopts the very allegorical and circular concept of "silence is an accelerator," anything and everything becomes permissible. This view of the "silence" issue is an open lid to a "Pandora's Box" of ever increasing error. It is the same view that King Saul took to justify his rebellion against the very clear and linear directive of God regarding the Amalekites in I Samuel 15

---

[164] See a list of 2008 participants at the Tulsa Workshop at: www.tulsaisww.com/id17. html

as we illustrated earlier. Over the centuries, Origen's allegorical interpretive method has in our day morphed into a post-modern circular interpretive model that provides no answers, only more questions. It enthusiastically asserts that "silence" is an accelerator. This "accelerator" sends people reeling towards "worshipping the creation instead of the Creator" as Paul so passionately warms us against in Romans chapter 1.

Even while we discuss the errors of Circular Interpretation, some among us may have already slid from bad interpretation to NO interpretation at all.

13. Unholy Alliance— The Unequal Yoke Is Upon Us

Terry Rush is the pulpit preacher for the Memorial Drive church of Christ in Tulsa, OK and is a major organizer of the annual Tulsa International Soul Winners Workshop. Bro. Rush stated on December 16, 2006 in an address entitled, "Jesus Calls Us to Courageous Doctrine", that the way to unity among us is to reject ALL hermeneutical principles. He would have us reject BOTH linear and circular sides of the Silence question.[165] In other words, bro. Rush wishes us to embrace the Post-Modern "there is no truth and we couldn't find it anyway if we tried" philosophy. He plainly states that we are in a "always searching-never finding" state, "I think that we are always in kindergarten in learning about what God has going on."[166] Towards the end of the address he further builds on this premise,

> Let's just see if we could do an improved job of learning from the Word, wrestling with the things we don't understand and somehow saying to each other, "While we

---

[165] Now taken off their website as of 04.17.08, there WAS audio sermons in the MP3 Format at: www.tulsaworkshop.org/Podcast/"Jesus Calls to Courageous Doctrine"

[166] Ibid.

are learning, while we are in kindergarten, I want you to know I love you. [167]

He attempts to justify his line of thought by illustrating that when one is overtaken in death, those with whom the deceased has disagreed now feel harmonious with one another. Recalling the funeral of a church member, Rush observes:

> When we met on the foothill of death it changed our doctrine. And I say to you that love shows up when life gets real and that harmony becomes more palatable to us the more rugged life gets and the more death is present the more we will find reason to pull together and band together to survive.[168]

Earlier the question was asked, "Does the silence of the Scripture give a green light to go beyond what is written?" Sadly, bro. Rush believes it does give a green light. In his own words:

---

[167] Ibid.

[168] Ibid.

You know that the Christian Church is not going to come to Tulsa and give up their instruments. And people, I want you to know that I don't think we ought to ask them (to do so) . . . People, I want to tell you something. I think that the Judgment Day, it's just _____ [unsavory word deleted] to me, that we tell people that God is against instrumental music and when we see it in the Old Testament and it doesn't discuss it in the New but it looks like it's in heaven and so you're going to have people in hell looking across the chasm and they went to hell because they used instrumental music and they (are) watch(ing) them use it in heaven. *I don't think so!*[169]

Bro. Rush articulates these radical views much more gingerly to the far less Emergent readership of the ***Christian Chronicle***. Note how he "takes the edge off" the above quotation for those who are less aware of his Emergent theology:

There is a growing hunger among Churches of Christ to freely study and practice the stable teachings of holy writ without restraint from some who may have quit studying but

---

[169]   Ibid. Emphasis mine RM

shifted to regulating. Such limitation, coincidentally, drives many preachers from the pulpit because they cannot in good conscience continue to parrot doctrines of our heritage which did not come from faithful study of the Word. [170]

What's the difference between the two quotes? Not much. Both quotes clearly indicate that bro. Rush finds biblical linear interpretation regarding the instrument as coming entirely from the "misinformed ignorance" of Stone, Campbell, *et. al.* The Emergents among us would have us believe that all "thus saith the Lord" reverence for the Holy Word of God is based not, on anything biblical, but solely upon eighteenth century Scottish Rationalism that influenced our Founding Fathers in both the Declaration and the Constitution. Such a view is little more than a blatant re-writing

---

[170] Terry Rush, Tulsa, Oklahoma as quoted in "Letters" to the Christian Chronicle, August, 2008, pg. 35 (NOTE: The context in which this quote is taken concerns a response to an interview in the previous edition of the paper with Bro. Denny Petrillo of Bear Valley. He at first commends Bro. Petrillo and then begins to speak "Emergently." Here is the first portion of the entire text: "I applaud Denny Petrillo's heart and work for preaching (Dialogue, Page 23, July). Too, I root for his effectiveness. I'm not sure his comment, "Many in Churches of Christ are no longer committed to Christ and the apostles," is accurate. From my experience, there is growing interest in such, yet strong traditions of men among us attempt to restrict the Word just as in Christ and the apostles' day." Quite often when backed into a theological corner, Emergents claim that they are being "taken out of context." To avoid such a claim, I've now included the ENTIRE quote for the readers complete objective overview.)

of the historical record. The linear view of Scripture is clearly illustrated all the way back to at least Genesis 2:16-17 where God clearly and linearly states a command with man clearly and linearly understanding and accepting it. Also, in I Samuel 15 we see where Samuel asks the rhetorical question, "What then is the bleating of the sheep I hear?" He understood the Word of God in a clear and linear way. Not only that, the linear view of Scripture was at the very heart and soul of the well meaning Protestant Reformation a full 150 years prior to the advent of Scottish Rationalism! Note what Kaiser has to say:

> Although the doctrines of *sola fide* and *sola gratia* ("by faith alone" and "by grace alone") constituted the *material* principle of the Protestant Reformation, the *formal* principle was *sola scriptura.* The norm for all doctrine was not to be found in tradition or in the church but in "Scripture alone." That was a reversal of the strategy for interpretation that had begun in the Western school of the church fathers. [171]

---

[171] Kaiser & Silva, *op cit,* pg. 270 AUTHORS NOTE: The Emergents among us have taken up another new mantra. Instead of referring to us as the "church of Christ" or "the church," they now are referring to us as "the Stone-Campbell Movement." God did not add me to a "movement," He added me to the church of Christ upon my baptism as He did the 1st 3,000 souls on the day of Pentecost!

It is crystal clear that long before there was such a thing as "Scottish Rationalism," Luther had, at least to some extent, a linear view of Scripture. Note what Luther has to say:

> The Holy Ghost, declared Luther, is the all-simplest writer that is in heaven or earth: therefore his words can have no more than one simplest sense, which we call the scriptural or literal meaning. [172]

In bro. Rush's view it seems to this writer, Stone and Campbell were still drunk, as it were, from the American War for Independence and incapable of independent and objective reasoning. Anyone today disagreeing with him (Rush) seem to him little more than dupes at best and vile hypocrites at worst who continually "regulate" others, "restrict the Word" and "parrot" the views of men now dead for well over 100 years. Notice that bro. Rush applies a 100% Thomistic approach to this question without referencing any Scripture to back his views leaving us with "better questions" but no answers.

---

[172] Kaiser & Silva, *op cit,* pg. 270 quoting Luther as quoted in Fredrick W. Farar, History of Interpretation, Banpton Lectures, 1885 (Grand Rapids, MI: Baker, 1961), pg. 329 NOTE: Luther tried to have things "both ways." On the one hand, he espoused a more linear interpretive view and on the other the more pragmatic approach of retaining and reforming Romanism. In the end, he compromised adopting the left side of the silence of the Scriptures question.

"Imagination" regarding the instrument over rides the Scriptures in both Old and New Testaments. [See "Appendix #1" for a biblical exegesis of the Emergents "aftermarket proof texts" regarding the use of the instrument.] Bro. Rush . . . please come home!

We cannot overemphasize the influence upon the Tulsa Workshop by those advocating Alexandrian/Allegorical/Circular/Thomistic / *Sensus Plenior* interpretive methods. Can error travel from The Fall to 2nd Century Alexandria to apostate Rome to the 21st Century cities of San Francisco, Nashville and Tulsa?

Truth IS indeed stranger than fiction, . . . ERROR IS A TIME TRAVELER.

Of course we know that only God transcends time. Satan's power is limited and he cannot transcend time. However, the same lie Satan told Adam and Eve is still being told today . . . with the same damning effect.

As we have noted, originated by Origen and perfected by Thomas Aquinas and Romanism over the centuries, allegorical interpretation has a long and sordid history. This error is once again raising its ugly head in our day. This neo-Gnostic circular approach to interpretation has infiltrated the Lord's church and is racing through the brotherhood virtually unchecked.

Circular Interpretation has at its core an allegorical foundation. An "allegory" to biblical interpretation is/are fictional story(s) assigned by the interpreter to "understand" the personal hidden message(s) contained within any given passage. As un-biblical as subjectively interpreting Scripture is, evil is compounded when allegorical stories are combined with the "undiscoverable truth" philosophy of post-modern man.

In the beginning, God spoke clearly, understandably and linearly with a singular message. For a time Adam and Eve clearly understood and obeyed that message without question; they "rightly divided the word of truth." Here is what God said;

> And the Lord God commanded the man, saying, "Of every tree of the garden you may freely eat; but of the tree of the knowledge of good and evil you shall not eat, for in the day that you do eat of it you shall surely die."—Genesis 2:16-17 (NKJV)

Things changed radically when an "out of town preacher" showed up with a "new slant" on the "interpretation" of Genesis 2:16-17! He "discovered" God's "disguised motivation" hidden between the lines of the text! Based upon this "story," He turned around and called God a liar! Here's the allegorical and circular interpretation of Genesis 2:16-17 preached by Satan:

> And the serpent said to the woman, "You will not surely die. For God knows that in the day you eat of it your eyes will be opened, and you will be like God, knowing good and evil.— Genesis 3:4-5 (NKJV)

There we have it, the father of allegorical and circular interpretation is none other than Satan himself. He prototypes here the circular interpretive model by assigning allegory to truth. The circular/Alexandrian/Circular/Emergent "interpreter" takes whatever God says clearly and asserts that the passage has multiple hidden meanings, illustrates the many hidden meanings with stories and finally concludes that the "truth" is OPPOSITE to the crystal clear, unambiguous, linear and original singular message spoken by the Holy Spirit. Paraphrasing Satan's circular approach,

I know it "says" that "on the day you shall eat of the fruit you shall surely die," but here's the real story. God is just concealing his hidden motivation here to protect his divine status. You see God doesn't want any competition from the likes of you! Here's the bottom line, you will NOT surely die and instead become god's like he is!

Where am I going with all of this? You "may" have someone (or several someone's) in your congregation who attended the 2008 Tulsa International Soul Winners Workshop. The most prominently displayed corporate sponsor in 2008 for the work shop was ZOE GROUP/NEW WINESKINS. When you go to the ZOE/Wineskins website[173] their new logo at the top has 4 buttons. For a short time during the spring of 2008 before it's removal, one found on the very first button, from left to right, an image of the champion of post-modern allegory, Brian McLaren. That button is entitled "Enrichment Conferences." Such a prominent display was a *de facto* endorsement of ALL that Brian McLaren teaches. [For reasons unknown, McLarens image has now been replaced with one of bro. Randy Harris.] We could keep listing McLaren's errors for weeks on end but suffice to say that Brian McLaren is not a Christian in

---

[173]   See www.zoegroup.org

the New Testament sense of the word, as stated emphatically several times in this book. You can still buy all of McLaren's books off the ZOE website. Here is what McLaren says regarding hell, God's motives and the death of Christ:

> One of the huge problems is the traditional understanding of hell. Because if the cross is in line with Jesus' teaching then—I won't say, the only, and I certainly won't say even the primary—but a primary meaning of the cross is that the kingdom of God doesn't come like the kingdoms of this world, by inflicting violence and coercing people. But that the kingdom of God comes through suffering and willing, voluntary sacrifice. But in an ironic way, the doctrine of hell basically says, no, that that's not really true. That in the end, God gets His way through coercion and violence and intimidation and domination, just like every other kingdom does. The cross isn't the center then. The cross is almost a distraction and false advertising for God.[174]

---

[174] From www.understandingthetimes.org/mclarentrans/shtml via www.bereanbeacon. org

To illustrate the brazen nature of his theology (nothing short of a total and complete denial and repudiation of Romans 3:25; Hebrews 2:17. I John 2:2 and I John 4:10) one has no need to go further than his statements regarding the purpose of the death of our dear Lord and Savior on the cross. PLEASE, don't take my word for it, check it out for yourselves. He concludes that "if" God actually allowed Christ to die for our sins it would be like you and I kicking the dog when we are angry! The exact quote: ". . . God is incapable of forgiveness unless he kicks someone else."[175] McLaren here is quoting a well known preacher who he does not name so as to "protect" him. However, these are clearly Brian McLaren's own sentiments. Brian McLaren, was one of the keynote speakers at the October, 2007 "ZOE Conference" in Nashville, TN. Other keynotes speakers included brothers Mike Cope, Randy Harris and Jeff Walling.[176]

So, just how does Brian McLaren view the churches of Christ?

---

[175] From www.youtube.com/Brian McLaren/Brian McLaren's Attack Against Hell and Jesus Atonement.

[176] See www.zoegroup/Enrichment Conferences/Conferences/Nashville, October, 2007

Why does he devote so much time and energy to a numerically insignificant body?

What possible purpose might he have for regularly "showing up" at our various conferences, lectureships and summits?

Bro. Phill Wilson, associated with the fully emerged Otter Creek Church (church of Christ) in Nashville, TN wrote about McLaren's views towards the Lord's church in October, 2007 after McLaren "consulted" with the Otter Creek "leadership" for several hours while in Nashville as quoted below. During that session, according to bro. Wilson's blog at the time, McLaren referred to the biblical teaching on acappella singing in worship as "stupid." [177] As noted often, Emergents "speak a different language" than faithful people do. Emergents love to turn semantical somersaults with language. Note an example:

> *Salvation* is another debated word. Before the days of the existentialists, salvation meant to be cleansed from sin by the blood of Christ [in baptism—RM] and given everlasting

---

[177] See jphilwilsonsblog.blogspot.com Posted October 12, 2007

life. It was essentially salvation from sin that came because of the work of Christ on Calvary.

The neoorthodox view has altered this. Salvation becomes basically a psychological experience with the personality of Jesus. It is a transforming relationship rather than a quickening from the dead.[178]

These word gyrations allow the Emergents to "seem faithful" without actually "being faithful" to God's Word. That being the case, [I have made some explanatory notes re-translating Emergent words and phrases back into English.] [RM]

McLaren talked about how Churches of Christ actually have a benefit in how they have been separate from the rest of the Christian world. He contends that much of the evangelical world is not caught up in the framing *story* (1) of the Kingdom of God. Rather, they have bought into the Imperialism *story,* (2) especially as they have associated themselves with particular political *stories.* (3) He called it a "membrane" between us and the rest of the Christian

---

[178] Dave Breese, *op cit,* pg. 220

world. Now, he didn't say that it's a bad thing that people like Max Lucado have been publicly associated with Churches of Christ and popular in the wider Christian world, but it does make the membrane thinner. McLaren feels (4) that some of the more progressive (5) Churches of Christ can speak very prophetically (6) to the wider Christian world about the message of Jesus, rather than buying into any of the other framing *stories*. (7) Now, notice that he's not calling for isolation (8) from the "denominations," but engagement. Rather than pull up our tents, we go out into the wider Christian world and call not for a restoration of the forms of the first century church, (9) but for a restoration of a community of people who are *seeking* (10) to become disciples of Christ. [179]

Allow me now to comment:

1. When McLaren speaks of the "framing story of the Kingdom of God," he is referring to his infamous quote already cited, ". . . the essential message of Jesus (is) compassion for yourself and

---

[179] Ibid. jwilsonsblog.blogspot.com. Posted October 12, 2007. NOTE: I have added numbers to reference my commentary below of this quote - RM

your fellow neighbor." This is the "core of the gospel" as he sees it. His "essential message" leaves God completely out and by default elevates the individual to "god" status as Paul warns against in Romans chapter 1. As *wikipedia.com* observes:

> A frame story (also frame tale, frame narrative, etc.) is a narrative technique whereby a main story is composed, at least in part, for the purpose of organizing a set of shorter stories, each of which is a story within a story—or for surrounding a single story within a story. This literary devise acts as a convenient *conceit* [In literary terms, a *conceit* is an extended metaphor (allegory—RM) with a complex logic (reason—RM) that governs an entire poem or poetic passage (or non-poetic—RM). By juxtaposing, usurping and and manipulating images and ideas in surprising ways, a *conceit* invites the reader into a more sophisticated understanding of an object of comparison.][180] for the organization of a set of smaller narratives which are either of the devising of the author, or taken from a previous

---

[180]   See http:/wikipedia.org/wiki/conceit, (Emphasis added—RM)

stock of popular tales slightly altered by the author for the purpose of the longer narrative. [181]

When Emergents speak of a "framing story" or a "narrative" what they are REALLY saying is this: "The Bible is true in the big picture sense but it is put together by many individual "stories" that have varying degrees of reliability, some are in fact completely false." As a result, people get to "pick and choose their own truth" from the pages of Scripture, living any way they wish while THINKING they are on their way to heaven. This falsehood seems vaguely similar (remember Solomon said that "there is nothing new under the sun?") to what Thomas Jefferson did in the early 19th century. His Deist error propelled him to cut out verses he didn't care for and publish what was left in what became known as *The Jefferson Bible:*

> *The Jefferson Bible* begins with an account of Jesus' birth without references to angels, genealogy, or prophesy. Miracles, references to the Trinity and the divinity of Jesus, and Jesus' resurrection are also absent . . . [182]

---

[181]   Ibid. See http://wikipedia.org/wiki/frame_story

[182]   See: http://wikipedia.org/wiki/jefferson_bible

I've just described the "framing story of the Kingdom of God" as Brian McLaren is actively teaching an ever growing number of our brethren. God help us. This radically circular form of biblical interpretation is used by McLaren as a vehicle to define good and evil in purely economic terms. [183]

Essentially, Brian McLaren allergorizes the Scriptures to the point that he "interprets" Genesis as would Karl Marx! To McLaren, evil in the world is defined, not by sin, but by capitalism and "over consumption" by Western economies. In other words, Brian McLaren has re-treaded 1970's Central and South American "liberation theology," where man no longer needs salvation from sin, but from economic exploitation from the United States and her allies in the world. In McLaren's thinking, Ronald Reagan is the villain and Che Guevara is the hero! The capitalist turns out to be the epitome of evil in the world and the socialist turns out to be the savior of the world.

---

[183]   Brian McLaren, Everything Must Change—Jesus, Global Crises, and a Revolution of Hope, (Thomas Nelson, Inc., Nashville, TN, 2007), pg. 209-210 as referenced by Chris Rosebrough's blog, "Extreme Theology." See more analysis at: http://extremetheology.com/2007/10/mclarens-new-bo-html.

2. McLaren refers here to the "imperialism story." The "imperialism story," in McLaren's mind, is the alleged cabal between denominational religion and "American Manifest Destiny." He sees churches of Christ somehow exempt from the "imperialism story," since we have historically stayed at "arms length" from the political scene in America, especially those who would emulate the views of David Lipscomb. I would say, however, that our non-political involvement in American politics is absolutely NOT an indication that we would automatically buy into radical socialism, especially the kind that Brian McLaren has for sale! McLaren apparently assumes because his ZOE contacts are theological leftists, that churches of Christ are ripe for not only leftist theology, that we can be further duped into leftist political movements and collectivist economic models. What a "leap of faith" on McLaren's part!

3. "Political stories" are a further extension of the "imperialism story" nonsense. McLaren sees the church of Christ as some kind of patsy for conservative political views. Now before you think I've gone too far here, may I remind you again that the Emergent's among us are continually trying to convince faithful people to buy into the absurd theory that men like Campbell and Stone were primarily influenced, not by the Bible, but by War for Independence

era Scotch-Irish rationalism. McLaren's view of the church of Christ is condescending, to say the least. Apparently, he sees us all as simpletons and dupes. In McLaren's mind if Campbell and Stone were duped by the teachings of Locke, Paine and Jefferson then we today are doubly duped. The fact that "faith cometh by hearing and hearing by the Word of God," is a truth that McLaren rejects outright and he is forced to come up with nonsense to explain to his confused mind the church of Christ.

4. McLaren, like other Post-Modernists rely on their emotions and "feelings" to lead them to what little "truth" that they may stumble onto.

5. "Progressive" is a code word for "Emergent." This is a classic example of when someone "spins" a "negative" into a "positive," *i.e.* the abortionist is not a "taker of life," he is a "giver of choice."

6. "Speaking prophetically" means, according to McLaren, that these so-called "progressive churches of Christ" can spread his "framing story of the the Kingdom of God" more efficiently than other religious bodies. Our past "isolationist" tendencies regarding denominationalism gives us some sort of twisted *gravitas*.

Churches of Christ could become the perfect "mole" to infiltrate Evangelicalism, no one would suspect US OF ALL PEOPLE! In other words since we refused in the past to have an "unequal yoke" with denominations, a sudden impulse to take on such a yoke would be seen as very useful to one who wanted to promote falsehood to the unsuspecting. The idea is sinister. Brian McLaren is attempting to co-opt the church of Christ for his own dubious purposes. Should you think my comment "beyond the pale," I have two words for you . . . Max Lucado, a man who is now promoting that which he once opposed. Bro. Lucado now possesses, not only *gravitas,* he appears to be coated with theological Teflon ®!

7. It is interesting to see that Brian McLaren, the worlds foremost advocate of multiple meaning allegorical interpretation of the Scripture lets something slip . . . some "stories" are superior to "other stories!" What a contradiction! Frankly, it is highly oxymoronic to say that any Post-Modern Emergent can "know" anything for they universally reject the concept of absolute truth. Truth to Brian McLaren is nebulous, elusive, un-obtainable and individually defined. Therefore, when he asserts that some "stories" are superior to "other stories," he proves himself to be a man who "dances between two opinions" as did the Israelites of Elijah's day!

8. Paul says in II Corinthians 6:14 that we should not be "unequally yoked with un-believers." Brian McLaren here, with his word "engagement," is advocating just that . . . and we must flee faster than Joseph ran from Potiphar's wife.

9. McLaren here is debunking the holy aspiration to be faithful to the New Testament in all things. He and the Emergents ridicule what they call "patternism." Sadly, the lessons of Korah's Rebellion, "written for our learning," go unheeded in the Emergent church.

10. As we mentioned early on, the "seeking of truth" is a noble enterprise to an Emergent while he proclaims the impossibility of success in such an effort. Taken to its logical conclusion, all sincere Muslims, Hindus, tree worshipers, denominationalists etc. will be saved as long as they are sincerely "seeking God." However, Jesus Christ asserted that "ye shall know the truth and the truth shall set you free," that God's Word is truth and through it we will be sanctified and the Holy Spirit would bring to the apostles memories all things that Jesus taught them. Those remembered teachings are

contained in the Gospels, the Acts, the Epistles and the Revelation. [See John 8:31-32; John 17:17 & John 14:26] [184]

McLaren possesses a rare skill set. He can speak in such a way as to allow his audience to hear . . . and believe . . . ANYTHING they want to! Such falsehood is so potent and deadly, I can't find words to describe it. I believe that Brian McLaren poses the greatest single threat to the church of Christ since Constantine. If the faithful do not wake up immediately, he and his allies will sweep away much of the church of Christ into apostasy within five years of today. Brian McLaren and his cohorts in the church are bringing his damnable doctrines into the church of Christ like a Trojan Horse.

I believe that Brian McLaren is focusing on the churches of Christ because we, as members of Christ's Body, strive daily to "rightly divide the Word of Truth" and are therefore "fully equipped" to resist error, including the Gnostic kind. McLaren will continue his infiltration of the faithful until he is opposed with overwhelming force . . . the faithfulness of you and me as God gives us strength!

---

[184] NOTE: My commentary section regarding what bro. Phil Wilson said on his blog regarding Brian McLaren is just that...commentary. Why? Simply this: Finding definitive quotes regarding what Brian McLaren REALY believes is just a little easier than nailing Jello ® to a wall with a power nail gun!

Not surprising, Brian McLaren has many allies in his campaign to allegorize the entire Word of God. One such ally is the radical and biblically agnostic cleric, Alan Jones of San Francisco. Jones is referred to as the "Very Reverend" Dean of the self-identified Grace Cathedral of Henry VIII's Anglican religion.

In addition to the usual cafeteria fare of worn out main line Protestant liberalism, Jones is outspoken in his support for something called the United Religions Initiative or U.R.I. The U.R.I. wants to unite the world's religions into one body and mandate their beliefs into international law. They want to become, as it were, an international dictatorship over religious thought and practice, sort of a United Nations for religion. Check it all out for yourself.[185] Many pine for a one-world government and a one-world economy. These same people are now beginning to clamor for a one-world religion. How convenient to tyranny! Mankind already tried and failed to voluntarily form a one-world system. You make recall that failed attempt at the Tower of Babel.

Jones has written a book called ***Reimagining Christianity— Reconnect Your Spirit Without Disconnecting Your Mind***, sort

---

[185] See www.uri.org

of a personal spiritual manifesto.[186] His beliefs are chilling to say the least. In the book he champions the prideful doubt and noble ignorance of a skeptic, the allegorical interpretive model of Origen, the elevation of Thomistic human reason over revealed truth. In addition, he openly rejects nearly everything sacred along with various and sundry other heretical errors. The danger of this man's teaching cannot be over stated! Essentially, Alan Jones is an agnostic masquerading as a cleric. His blatant and rebellious UNBELIEF is clearly articulated by what he says in his book. He is a true post-modern disciple of Origen's allegorical interpretive model and the "reason over revelation" teachings of thirteenth century Thomas Aquinas. Here are two illustrative quotes:

From the very beginning when I heard those Bible *stories*, I believed them in a *mystical* way—as a way of communicating deep truths by way of *images*. I *instinctively* read the Bible as *allegory and metaphor, not as literal truth.*[187]

. . . about the *stories* of the Bible. Are they to be trusted? If so, in what way? Are the words attributed to Jesus in the

---

[186]   Alan Jones, *op. cit.*

[187]   Alan Jones, *op. cit.* pg. 14 (XIV) as cited by Richard Bennet via www.bereanbeacon. org. Emphasis mine RM.

New Testament really his? My approach has always been *skeptical with regard to the text* and open with regard to the tradition . . . I don't believe that what we can know of Jesus is confined to the New Testament. We have 2,000 years of *experience* and worship to draw on . . . we can get to the truth only by inference . . . through *myth and poetry*, through *metaphor and story telling.* There is no such thing as "what really happened." That's why history is always being rewritten.[188]

It would be refreshing if, at least, radical theologians could be original! Jones' sentiments are strikingly similar to the late agnostic theologian, Julius Wellhausen who ended his life believing virtually none of the Holy Bible. Please note:

According to Wellhausen, then, some passages, including all of Deuteronomy, were written as a result of an evolutionary process and not by divine revelation.

---

[188] Ibid. pgs. 209-210 as cited by Richard Bennet via www.bereanbeacon.org. Emphasis mine RM.

Wellhausen regarded Israel's history prior to the beginning of the monarchy of Israel as uncertain. Exodus, he thought, was completely historical; prior to that, all was myth.

Wellhausen's scholarship became an important contribution to liberalism as it sought to demythologize the Bible by taking God and spiritual things out of it. Through this means, Wellhausen opened the door for subsequent scholars [Jones, McLaren, *et al*—RM] to expand the base of liberalism and add to it their own interpretations of biblical truth. Some found the Bible to be an endless round of allegories rather than necessary historical truth. [189]

Alan Jones had a radio broadcast before his retirement called "The Forum." He had McLaren as a regular guest AND McLaren often spoke during the liturgy! [Audio MP3's of McLaren's sermons are available for listening on the Grace Cathedral website noted below] Jones was so fond of McLaren that McLaren's image was prominently displayed on the website.[190]

---

[189]   Dave Breese, *op cit,* pg. 95
[190]   See www.gracecathedral.org/The Forum

Now, here is Brian McLaren who is "instructing" the Lord's people in Nashville and Abilene while hobnobbing with Anglicans (radical Anglicans at that!) in San Francisco at the same time! How is that possible? It is NOT possible . . . unless . . . The ZOE Group, ALONG WITH ALL THOSE THAT SUPPORT THEM, are UNEQUALLY YOKED WITH UNBELIEVERS!

> Do not be unequally yoked with unbelievers. For what *FELLOWSHIP* has righteousness with lawlessness? And what *COMMUNION* has light with darkness? And what *ACCORD* has Christ with Belial? Or what *PART* has a believer with an unbeliever? And what *AGREEMENT* has the temple of God with idols? For you are the temple of the living God.—II Corinthians 6:14-16a (NKJV) [Emphasis mine RM] [191]

ZOE Group and Alan Jones/Grace Cathedral, via Brian McLaren, have formed *A FELLOWSHIP, A COMMUNION, AN ACCORD, A PART AND AN AGREEMENT* regarding the interpretation of the Scriptures. This poison was injected into the church of Christ by

---

[191] See Appendix #2 for an exegetical outline of the entire context of this critical passage.

way of ZOE's sponsorship of the Tulsa International Soul Winners Workshop in March, 2008. The un-equal yoke carried by the Tulsa Workshop conspiring *vis-à-vis* with ZOE Group conspiring *vis-à-vis* with Brian McLaren conspiring *vis-à-vis* with Alan Jones must be broken—and soon—in order for us to avoid a new apostasy.

Lest any of us doubt that the ZOE Group is in the aggressive process of abandoning the "faith once for all delivered to the saints" in favor of the Platonic philosophies of Jones and McLaren, we need go no further than the published sentiments of bro. Greg Taylor, *Senior Editor of **New Wineskins**. Here are several quotes that show that bro. Taylor is clearly in the Jones-McLaren camp, and is pining for the rest of us to join him:

> Leaving one Christian church for another Christian church is not the same as leaving Christ or the truth.[192]

> So my wife and I believe and teach our children that we are part of the larger body of Christ, and that God is much bigger than Churches of Christ and the Stone-Campbell

---

[192] Greg Taylor, "The 21st Century Restoration-Will We Join It?" New Wineskins, March-April, 2008.

Movement. I know this is no news to many reading this, but I also believe what I'm about to say will challenge all of us in the Stone-Campbell family. We want to fellowship with and participate in the life of Christians worldwide and in various denominations.[193]

Our worldview is different from the typical of two or three generations of Churches of Christ. For example, my ten-year-old daughter asked, "What's the difference between that Methodist church and ours?" I said there are no differences important enough to explain right now. "Both believe Jesus is the God's Son and the Holy Spirit lives in us."[194]

The world is changing and our worldview ought also to change. Rather than asking, "Are the Baptists or the Catholics right?" millions are asking a question on a completely different plane: "Is Jesus the Lord or should I follow Muhammad?" I'm more concerned to tell Muslims and sinners about Jesus than I am debating matters of precise doctrinal formulations with fellow Christians. I'd

---

[193]   Ibid.
[194]   Ibid.

rather show a wanderer the gospel of Jesus than "convert" an Episcopalian's view of scripture to mine.[195]

Question, "IF" Baptists, Catholics, Methodists and Anglicans are saved, and saved in RADICALLY diverse ways, how can bro. Taylor then turn to the Muslim and "sinner" and tell them that THEY are NOT saved?" There are "good Muslims" and "good sinners" everywhere one turns. Again, some may think these conclusions too rash. We, unfortunately, already have evidence that bro. Taylor's words are having their desired effect:

judaism, christianity, and islam all worship the same deity. division and "restoration" are an intrinsic quality of all religions and if you are truly faithful to whatever you believe in then the search for perfect communion in your own life will never be attained. there really is no need to splinter away from any congregation unless it hinders your mission. you may not believe it but muslims and christians have quite a bit in common. if you decide to have a dialog

---

[195]   Ibid.

with an islamic scholar your idea of islam will likely shock you in retrospect.—Anonymous [196]

The response is mortifyingly instructive. Bro. Taylor limits his "new restoration" appeal to so-called "Christians" in "other denominations." The commenting respondent takes bro. Taylor's sentiments and takes them "to the next level" . . . to the pagan religions. Illustrative of the progressive nature of this error going straight into the church of Christ is this recent quote from the *Christian Chronicle*. Here an unidentified preacher relays the comments from an unidentified member in his audience:

> Recently, I had a thoughtful individual at the church where I preach approach me in strict confidence to talk about some thoughts he has. He still believed Jesus is the only way to heaven, but he is considering whether everyone will *know* that they were saved by Jesus. In other words, many Muslims might make it to heaven by the grace of God and the saving power of Jesus, even though they don't know it. [197]

---

[196] Ibid./Comments/NOTE: I have left this quote intact as it was originally written. Post-modern people, consistent with their "no obtainable truth" belief system, habitually do not use capital letters.

[197] Bobby Ross, "Survey: Americans See Many Routes to Eternal Life," Christian Chronicle, August, 2008, pg. 4 (***Author's Note: Whether or not this person is a***

Total doubt and confusion regarding the saving gospel of our Lord and Savior Jesus Christ is where bro. Taylor's teaching will take ALL OF US unless the clear, unambiguous, linear and understandable Word of God is boldly proclaimed once more from our pulpits.

Where will it all end? It will end when the Taylor/McLaren/Jones vision of "inter-faith unity" is achieved by adding the church of Christ to the list of panelists below. Every major city has some kind of "inter-faith" organization. In Charlotte it is Charlotte—Mecklenburg Ministries. Here is an announcement of one of their recent meetings:

> Unity or Disunity: Is Faith Bringing Us Together or Dividing Us Apart in Charlotte?

♦ How do you keep true to your religious beliefs while participating in interfaith activities?

Christian or not, we don't know. Christian or not, won't you pray with me for this person and this brother so the truth can be clearly taught and understood? "Father in heaven: We praise You and thank You for creating the man in the quote. We ask that You be with the brother that preaches that let us know of this persons doubts. We pray that You will strengthen and embolden this preacher of Your Word to pray and study with this man until faith is either established or restored in his heart. We pray for blessings on all the families involved. In Jesus Name; AMEN")

- What are the issues that divide us but which we are afraid to discuss?

- What is a realistic vision for next steps for Charlotte's faith community?

PANELISTS:

- Imam Khalil Akbar—Masjid Ash Shaheed

- Rev. Russ Dean—Park Road Baptist Church

- Rabbi Murray Ezring—Temple Israel

- Dr. Clifford Jones—Friendship Missionary Baptist Church

- Moderator: Rabbi Judy Schindler—Temple Beth El

These interfaith panelists will discuss the change they have seen in the faith community in Charlotte. They will also vulnerably and honestly discuss: where in the faith community are there sources of:

- Unity—where faith is pulling us together

- Disunity—where faith is driving us apart[198]

Though the above is both strange and bizarre to a faithful Christian, it is quite reflective of the "man on the street." The Jones/McLaren/Taylor *et al* vision of universal salvation, multiple meaning interpretive methods and a doubtful and skeptical view of the Holy Bible is nearly realized among the general population and they long to bring the church of Christ into this house of error as well. The sentiments of the general population are verified by a Pew Forum on Religion & Public Life poll released on June 23, 2008. According to the Pew analysis, Americans who claim a religious affiliation believe that salvation is obtainable outside of Christ, that there are multiple "true" ways to interpret and Bible and that the Bible may not be the inerrant Word of God. Note the following quotes from Pew's own analysis:

A major survey by the Pew Research Center's Forum on Religion & Public Life finds that most Americans have a non-dogmatic approach to faith. A majority (70%) of those

---

[198] From www.meckmin.org

affiliated with a religion, for instance, do not believe their religion is the only way to salvation.

And almost the same number (68%) believes that there is more than one true way to interpret the teachings of their religion.

A similar pattern is evident in the views of the Bible. Nearly two-thirds of the public (63%) takes the view that their faiths sacred texts are the Word of God. But those who believe Scripture represents the Word of God are roughly evenly divided between those who is should be interpreted literally (33%) and those who say it should not be taken literally (27%). [199]

Should these ghastly trends remain unchallenged, we will all wind up locked arm in arm, as it were, with John Lennon . . . who was just "somewhat" to the left of Alan Jones and Brian McLaren. We will be swaying to and fro as we sing the words to the all too familiar atheist refrain, the logical extension of the "imagination theology" of Thomas Aquinas:

---

[199]   See: http://religions-pewforum.org/pubs/876/religion-america-part-two containing the Pew Forum on Religion and Public Life—Religious Beliefs and Practices/Social and Political Views: Report 2, June 23, 2008.

Imagine there's *no heaven*

It's easy if you try

No hell below us

Above us only sky[200]

Yes, it is true. Travel with Jones, McLaren, Taylor *et al* and you will wind up with John Lennon as your spiritual mentor, the man who once claimed to be more popular than our Lord Jesus Christ Himself. Yes. Thomas Aquinas would be very proud of his Post-Modern student, the late John Lennon—spiritual advisor to millions who would rather IMAGINE truth than to HEAR it!

The time travel route of error is now clear:

From Satan to Plato to Philo to Clement to Origen to Aquinas to Wellhausen to Alan Jones to Brian McLaren to Greg Taylor to *New Wineskins* to the ZOE Group to the Tulsa International Soul Winning Workshop to _____?

Satan wants to fill in the blank with your name and mine, the name of your congregation and mine.

---

[200]   See: www.oldielyrics.com

The common thread of this time traveling error is the allegorical interpretation of God's Word, prototyped at the Fall and still working today. We must, with truth and love, oppose these false teachers. More importantly,

We must down load the inerrant, revealed, clear, unambiguous and linear Word of God into our minds and hearts daily and rededicate ourselves to our primary mission of making disciples, baptizing and teaching all things that Jesus taught in the Gospels, the Acts, the Epistles and the Revelation.

The very *linear* words of the Psalmist in #119 come to mind:

Blessed are the undefiled in the way, who *walk* in the law of the Lord. Blessed are they that *keep* his testimonies. They also do no iniquity, they *walk* in his ways. Thou hast commanded us to *keep* to keep thy precepts diligently. O, that my ways were *directed* to keep thy statutes! Then I shall not be ashamed when I have respect unto all thy commandments. I will praise thee with uprightness of heart when I shall have *learned* thy righteous judgments. I will *keep* thy statutes, O forsake me not utterly.—Psalm 119, Section "A-Lepth"/[Emphasis mine RM](KJV)

We all should heed the words of the wisdom of Proverbs 30:6; "Add thou not unto his words, lest he reprove thee, and thou be found a liar." (KJV) Forcing the inspired Word of God into non-ending circular nonsense is nothing short of "adding unto his words." The GOOD NEWS is that the Scriptures themselves instruct us in proper biblical interpretation.

14. BIBLICAL INTERPRETATION "BY THE BOOK!"

We have spent a great deal of time on Alexandrian/Circular style interpretive methods. On the other hand, BIBLICAL interpretive methodology is *linear,* Antiochene (Antioch, Syria) theology is *linear,* Linear interpretation discovers that any particular passage has an essential original single meaning. Linear theology proclaims that the original meaning of the author IS knowable and important, that truth is discoverable within God's revealed Word and that truth is to be held corporately. The best way to define the linear or Antiochene interpretive method is this: any given passage holds a single original meaning communicated from the Holy Spirit to the author and from the author to his audience. This single original meaning is discoverable by examining period history, the text, the context, the grammar and even the words themselves . . . all in concert. Finally, when the original meaning and intent is discovered, then proper application to our own day and time is then possible. Linear theology is just what it states, there is a beginning point . . . the question . . . and there is a finish point . . . the answer.

I spoke of Alexandrian/Origenian/*sensus plenior*/Circular/Multiple Meaning interpretive methods historically and philosophically for they have no basis in Scripture. NOW I will speak of and define biblical (linear) interpretation using ONLY Scripture.

Far more important than mere philosophical questions, how does the Scripture view Scripture, linearly or circularly? Is the Word of God clear or is it ambiguous? Does the Bible presuppose divine revelation or does it presuppose the "noble ignorance" of post-modernism? Does the Bible invite us to knowledge or confusion?

You will hear Emergents speak with condescension and derision towards the entire subject of hermeneutics. They would have you and I believe that the study of hermeneutics is outdated, antiquated and part of the dust of history. They would have us believe that anyone who would study and then apply hermeneutical principles is somehow less than intelligent, unable to think for themselves and are being duped by unseen 3rd parties. The truth, however, is a stark contrast.

EVERYONE who attempts to study and/or teach the Scriptures has a hermeneutical approach, even the skeptic, even the unbeliever AND even the Emergent!

The very word proves this point. Liddell & Scott define the Greek verb *hermeneuo* as meaning "to interpret or explain" and define the Greek noun *hermeneia* as meaning "interpretation" and "explanation."[201] It is instructive to note that the Emergents, not acknowledging the existence of any standard of objective and obtainable truth, are loath to cite Scripture regarding any point. They do so reluctantly, hesitatingly and circularly. However, God's Word has MUCH to say regarding interpretive principles, though the actual word "hermeneutic" does not appear in the Holy Writ.

God gave Moses the Law and the Holy Spirit inspired him to write the first five books of the Bible. He also inspired many of the "prophets" and the "writings." All of these books constituted the "canon" to the Hebrew nation pre-exile. Post-exile, God used Ezra, Nehemiah and others in addition to the earlier prophets to both read AND interpret the Scripture to the returning exiles. For

---

[201] Henry George Liddell and Robert Scott, A Greek-English Lexicon, 9th ed. (1940), I, 690, (As quoted in Mickelsen's Interpreting the Bible, pg. 3) See Note #99 below.

all intents and purposes, Ezra, Nehemiah and certain Levites were the first to apply hermeneutics as we understand hermeneutics today. Their challenge, as is ours, was to take a foreign language and translate it to the point of understanding on the part of people ignorant of the original language. These men constituted the very first "hermeneutical team" to "take to the field." Prior to the exile, all Israel spoke, read and understood Hebrew, the language of God's people. However, during the exile the Israelis spoke, read and wrote in Aramaic, the language of their captors. Upon returning to the Promised Land, the returning exiles were re-exposed to God's Word for,

". . . in the post-exilic period the interpreter of the Old Testament had to translate the original Hebrew text into Aramaic and then explain the meaning . . . joined with oral discourse."[202]

The key point of all this is that Ezra, Nehemiah *et al* exercised hermeneutical services to the people of God by INSPRIATION! No man-made reasoning here! Note the following references bringing us the details of this first hermeneutical team:

---

[202]   Mickelsen, *op. cit.*, p. 22

- Ezra 7:6—Ezra was a biblical scholar.

- Ezra 7:11—Ezra was a legal scholar.

- Ezra 7:12—Ezra was a skilled transcriber.

- Ezra 7:21—Ezra was an ambassador of King Artaxerxes.

- Nehemiah 8:9—Nehemiah was the governor, Ezra was the priest and scribe and the Levites *taught the people.*

- Nehemiah 8:1—The people had a desire to hear the Word of God and asked Ezra the scribe to bring it to them.

- Nehemiah 8:2—The assembly noted in 8:1 was composed of men, women and children who could hear and understand words.

- Nehemiah 8:3—The Law of God was read from "early morning until midday" and "the ears of all the people were attentive to the Book of the Law." (NKJV)

- Nehemiah 8:4—Ezra stood on a wooden podium to address the people. Standing with him were six Levites on his right and seven Levites on his left.

- Nehemiah 8:5-6—Being above the people, Ezra opened the Book of the Law in the sight of all the people. As he opened it, all the people stood up. Ezra "blessed the Lord, the great God." (NKJV) All the people answered, "Amen! Amen! while lifting up their hands." (NKJV) All the people bowed their heads and worshipped God with their faces to the ground.

- Nehemiah 8:7—The 14 men of God (Nehemiah + the 13 Levites) "helped the people to understand the law." (NKJV) All the while, the people remained where they were.

- Nehemiah 8:8—Here is what the 14 men of God did that day: 1) They read from the Book of the Law and did so *clearly.* 2) They *gave the sense* and "helped the people understand the reading." (NKJV)

CONCLUSION: The biblical hermeneutic practiced by Ezra and his contemporaries, *under the inspiration of the Holy Spirit,* consisted of studious preparation, clear translation, clear reading and complete exposition of what was read. This model resulted, as it always will, in a complete understanding on the part of the congregation. The interpretive pattern was linear, clear and unambiguous. The delivered message was rendered in an expository fashion and had its desired effect.

According to denominational scholar A. Berkley Mickelsen,

. . . the task of interpreters of the Bible is to find out the meaning of a statement (command, question) for the author and for the first hearers or readers, and thereupon to transmit that meaning to modern readers. [203]

God's Word speaks for itself and asserts loudly, clearly and linearly in this regard:

Matthew 21:42-43—Jesus asks rhetorically, "have you not read the Scriptures?"

---

[203] Ibid. p. 5

LINEAR PRINCIPLE—Jesus asks a direct question, quotes a direct passage and makes a clear conclusion.

Matthew 22:29-30—Jesus clearly asserts that the Sadducees are WRONG, that they don't know the Scriptures nor do they know the power of God.

LINEAR PRINCIPLE—Wrong conclusions come from ignorance of the Scriptures which leads to error.

John 5:46—Jesus said, "If you believed Moses, you would believe me for he wrote of me."

LINEAR PRINCIPLE—There WAS a SINGULAR Moses, he wrote of Jesus and Jesus is the incarnate proof of BOTH his own claims to Deity and Kingship, as well as the veracity of the first 5 books of the Old Testament.

Luke 24:25-27—Jesus says the people were "foolish" not to believe, Jesus began with Moses and ALL the prophets and INTERPRETED to them all that the Scriptures said about himself.

LINEAR PRINCIPLE—Being slow of heart to believe the prophets is foolish. The prophets CAN be interpreted correctly for they spoke of Jesus

a. Gen. 3:15—He (Jesus) will bruise your (Satan's) head.

b. Gen. 12:3—In you (Jesus via Abraham's seed) all nations shall be blessed.

c. Gen. 22:18—In your offspring (Jesus) shall all the nations of the earth be blessed.

d. Num. 21:9 & John 3:14-15—"As Moses lifted up the serpent in the wilderness, so must the Son of Man be lifted up.

e. Num. 24:17—"I see him (Jesus) but not now; I behold him (Jesus) but not near; a star (Jesus) shall come out of Jacob, and a scepter (Jesus) shall rise out of Israel."

f. II Sam. 7:12-16—"He (Jesus) shall build a house for my name and I will establish the throne of his (Jesus) kingdom forever."

g. Isa. 7:14—"Behold a virgin shall conceive and bear a son, and shall call his name Immanuel." (God with us)

h. Isa. 9:6—For to us a child (Jesus) is born, to us a son (Jesus is given.

i. Isa. 50:6—I (Jesus) gave my back to those who strike, and my (Jesus) cheeks to those who pull out the beard.

j. Isa. 52:13-53:12—The Lord has laid on him (Jesus) the iniquity of us all . . . Yet it was the will of the Lord to crush him (Jesus)

k. Isa. 61:1 & Luke 4:18-19—The Spirit of the Lord is upon me (Jesus), because the Lord has anointed me (Jesus) to bring good news to the poor . . .

l. Jer. 23:5—I will raise up for David a righteous Branch (Jesus) and he (Jesus) will reign as king . . .

m. Dan. 7:13-14—There came one like the Son of Man (Jesus) . . . and to him (Jesus) was given dominion and glory and a kingdom, that all peoples, nations and languages should serve him (Jesus) . . .

n. Micah 5:2—But you, O Bethlehem Ephrathah . . . from you shall come forth for me one (Jesus) who is to be ruler in Israel . . .

o. Zech. 9:9— . . . behold, your king (Jesus)is coming to you; righteous and having salvation is he (Jesus), humble and mounted on a donkey, on a colt, the foal of a donkey.

p. Zech. 12:10— . . . when they look on me (Jesus), on him (Jesus) whom they have pierced, they shall mourn for him (Jesus) . . .

Luke 24:32—Jesus "opened up the Scriptures" on the road to Emmaus

LINEAR PRINCIPLE—The word "opened" is synonymous with "interpreted" to the point that their hearts BURNED within them!

Luke 24:45-46—Jesus "opened their minds to understand the Scriptures." He then said to them, "Thus it is written . . .:

LINEAR PRINCIPLE—Jesus interpreted the Scriptures and they UNDERSTOOD them.

John 5:39-40—Jesus clearly asserts that the Scriptures "bear witness about me."

LINEAR PRINCIPLE—The Scriptures as so clear as to ascend to the status of LEGAL PROOF in a court of law!

Acts 17:2—Paul "reasoned" with the Thessalonians "from the Scriptures, explaining and proving that is was necessary for the Christ to suffer and rise from the dead . . ."

LINEAR PRINCIPLE—The revealed Word of God is the basis for ALL reason and proof regarding those things spiritual.

Acts 17:11—The Bereans "searched the Scriptures daily to see whether these things were so."

LINEAR PRINCIPLE—The Scriptures are as to things spiritual as Blackstone is to things legal . . . the ultimate authority!

Acts 18:28—"(Paul) powerfully refuted the Jews in public, showing by the Scriptures that the Christ was Jesus."

LINEAR PRINCIPLE—The Scriptures are the ultimate refutation source of things in error.

Romans 15:4—Whatever was written "beforetime" was written for our learning . . . through the encouragement of the Scriptures we have hope."

LINEAR PRINCIPLE—Paul codifies the entire Old Testament as a inspired text book.

I Corinthians 15:3-4—According with the Scriptures, Jesus was buried and rose again on the 3rd day.

LINEAR PRINCIPLE—The Old Testament prophesies are now historical realities!

II Timothy 3:14-16—ALL Scripture is God Breathed and profitable for (all) teaching, (all) reproof, (all) correction and (all) training in righteousness.

> LINEAR PRINCIPLE—ALL Scripture comes from God and ALL Scripture is obtainable, understandable and adequate to EVERY spiritual need! God does not leave us to wander in circles searching for that which we cannot discover!

II Peter 3:15-16—Some Scriptures are hard to understand (linearly) and some take these Scriptures and "twist them to their own destruction."

> LINEAR PRINCIPLE—Hard to understand Scriptures are used by some to TWIST into CIRCULAR THEOLOGY to their own destruction. We observe that when one "twists," one does so in a circular motion, as in "circular interpretation." The irony is striking.

We must pause before leaving the subject of biblical interpretation to look at two passages that bring a profound sobriety to mind.

These passages, both given to Paul by the Holy Spirit, emphasize the deadly serious nature of our great commission.

II Timothy 2:15—"Be diligent to present yourself approved to God, a worker who does not need to be ashamed, rightly dividing the word of truth." (NKJV) Presenting oneself "to God" is a most solemn consideration. However, we need not be ashamed IF we, as Paul says "rightly divide the word of truth." The phrase "rightly dividing" comes from the single Greek word, *orthotomeo.* Literally, this word means "cutting straight."[204] It is a unique word, used only this time in the entire New Testament. According to ***Vine,*** *orthotomeo* ". . . passed from the idea of cutting or dividing, to the more general sense of rightly dealing with a thing. What is intended here is not dividing Scripture form Scripture, but teaching Scripture accurately."[205] Mickelsen cites a number of sources regarding the meaning of this phrase:

---

[204] As translated in the Nestle Greek Text with a Literal English Translation Copyrighted as Literal English Translation by Samuel Bagster and Sons Ltd. 1958 and contained in: The R.S.V. Interlinear Greek-English New Testament (London: Zondervan via Samuel Bagster and Sons, Ltd., 1968, 4th printing, 1972) p. 838

[205] W. E. Vine, M.A. An Expository Dictionary of New Testament Words with their Precise Meanings for English Readers (Old Tappan, New Jersey, Fleming H. Revell, Company, 1940, 17th Impression 1966) p. 327

Walter Bauer—"Guiding the word of truth along a straight path."

R. St. John Parry—". . . the figure may be of a stone mason who cuts stones straight and fair and straight to fit into their places in a building."

Moulton & Milligan—". . . to teach the word aright."

Spicq—" . . . to set forth [the message of truth] correctly and exactly . . ."

Latin Vulgate—*recte tractantem*—"handling rightly"[206]

When I soberly consider these observations, I can think first of no other Scripture than James 3:1—"Let not many of you become teachers, my brethren, knowing that as such we will incur a stricter judgment." (NASB) How can such precise language as Paul makes use of in I Timothy 2:15 have anything to do with the lowest of all standards of biblical analysis, circular interpretation? Sadly, for our

---

[206] Mickelsen, op. cit., pg. 4, Footnote #2

erring emergent brethren, it can have absolutely nothing to do with such a low standard as Paul makes clear:

> II Corinthians 2:17—"Unlike so many, we do not peddle the Word of God for profit. On the contrary, in Christ we speak before God with sincerity, like men sent from God." (NIV)

As "men sent from God," we are called to a much higher standard regarding God's word. What we do is not a retail or service product to be "spun" for a pragmatic larger pay off. Why? Because when we speak in Christ, we do so in the sight of God. This thought brings to mind the Scriptural warning, "Knowing therefore the terror of the Lord we persuade men . . ."—II Corinthians 5:11a (KJV)

God help us all if we fail to handle His Word with Precision, Care and Respect!

The Scriptural and linear approach to the subject of biblical interpretation is appropriately summarized by Bro. J. D. Thomas, past head of the ACU Bible Department:

To return to the principles of interpretation of the Restoration Movement, we remember that we have always believed that pattern authority was established by commands (or express statements); [Matthew 15:3-9; Mark 10:3-8] by necessary inference; [Matthew 22:29:32] and by approved precedents or approved apostolic examples. [Matthew 12:3-7] [207]

The Emergents among us are quick to ridicule what they call "patternism." They scoff at the very thought that God's Word is in any way, shape, matter or from is a "rule book" and that it has a "pattern." Bro. Edwards adeptly points out that I Cor. 14:27-31 contains "at least" six "rules" regarding the speaking of tongues in the 1st century Corinthian church before "that which is perfect has come." [208] Besides, EVERYTHING that God created is precise, orderly, predictable and has a distinct PATTERN about it! Why should the WORD OF GOD be the ONLY exception to the ULTIMATE ORDER that is the universe?! For Emergents to "assume" the Word of God is NOT a pattern, is tantamount to the

---

[207] Earl D. Edwards, "The Core Hermeneutic," in the Spritual Sword, journal article, October, 2001, pg. 10 quoting J. D. Thomas from his 1958 book, We Be Brethren. [Scriptures added—RM]

[208] Ibid., pg. 10

same logic used by the evolutionists who claim, in essence, that you and I came "from goo by way of the zoo!" Not only that, the Emergents mock the whole idea of such a thing as the Restoration Movement. They claim, as we speak elsewhere of, that the Restoration Movement is simply a historical/cultural/ philosophical event stuck in the early to mid 19th century. Their mocking is in vain. Let me make this point perfectly clear: the Restoration Movement was begun, not by Stone and Campbell, but by the Apostle Paul in the very 1st chapter of I Corinthians! There he urged the "denominations" of Corinth to abandon their sectarian ways and return to the teachings of the apostles! In an e-mail exchange with the author, bro. Terry Wheeler observes:

> The Corinthian Christians were determined to do "their own thing" and Paul's point is, "No." You get to do what all the other churches get to do. You do not get to go your own way. What Paul teaches the Corinthians is what he teaches all the churches, uniformity according to pattern. [209]

---

[209] From e-mails exchanged during the week of August 18, 2008. Bro. Wheeler references: I Corinthians 1:2; 4:6, 14-17; 11:2; 14:33, 37: 16:1 in support of his statement.

My friends, the Restoration Movement is nearly as old as the church of Christ itself! EVERY generation must have its own Restoration Movement. We are certainly no exception!

It is most interesting to note that both neo-Gnosticism and Alexandrian thought were believed to be long dead until our own very recent time when McLaren and other Emergents began dusting them off and repackaging them. It is also interesting to note that no congregation in the history of Christianity had more long term effect on world evangelism than did the Antioch church of Christ! Beginning with the sending of Paul and Silas, that congregation sent missionaries out for literally 100's of years and had lasting influence because theologically, they "rightly divided the word of truth" more diligently and for a longer time than most any other ancient congregation, setting the standard for the faithful church of that time. The faithful church in all subsequent times, ours included, owes the church of Christ of Antioch of Syria a great deal. May God be praised for their ancient diligence and faithfulness that lives on today![210]

---

[210] For a more in depth review of this amazing congregation, see "Antioch—A Church of Christ—Acts 11:19-30" by David Pharr in the March, 2008 issue of Carolina Messenger, page 4

15. The Emergent-Cy Among Us

As to churches of Christ and "Emergent Theology," **answers.com** said this;

> (They are) exploring long held beliefs within the 20th century Restoration heritage, (have) a network of weblogs (blogs) and have a common interest in providing ways for people to belong, identify with, and participate in the *conversation*, the community & Mission at varying levels.[211]

If there is any "portal" to "Emergent Theology" among our erring emergent and post-emergent brethren, it is **ZOEgroup.org.,** already discussed. ZOEgroup.org is a "not for profit" retail/promotional website that owns and publishes the *New Wineskins* magazine.[212] The Zoe Group and *New Wineskins* are the center of the universe, as it were, for emergent churches of Christ. Note what is stated

---

[211]   answers.com—See note #2/Emphasis mine RM

[212]   New Wineskins Magazine: Publisher: Larry Bridgesmith; Senior Editor: Mike Cope; Senior Editor Emeritus: Rubel Shelly; Managing/Senior Editor: Greg Taylor; Associate Editor: Sara Barton; Editors at Large: John Orgen, Thom Lemmons, Darryl Tippens, Lynn Anderson; Webservant: Keith Brenton; Executive Director, The ZOE Group, Inc.: Eric Noah-Wilson. See: wineskins.org/about us

on the ZOE Group web site regarding, in part, how they describe themselves:

> The ZOE Group provides resources to help God's people improve in the discipline of worship. Through the prophetic word, music, arts, drama and the gifts God has given his people in every age it is our prayer that excellence in the worship experience can be enhanced and improved, practiced and taught.[213]

And

> We are Christians only but not the only Christians and gladly add this ministry to the thousands of ministries worldwide that give glory and honor to God. [214]

As noted previously, ZOEgroup.org/*New Wineskins* is unequally yoked with Brian McLaren who is allied with the agnostic cleric, Alan Jones. Unfortunately, McLaren's influence is touted openly by many among us. Two notable examples are previously cited Wade

---

[213] Ibid.
[214] Ibid.

Hodges, the "senior minister" at the Garnett church of Christ, Tulsa, Oklahoma, and Greg Taylor, the Managing/Senior Editor of *New Wineskins Magazine* and assistant minister to Wade Hodges.

First of all, here is what Wade Hodges thinks of Brian McLaren in a blog quote after attending a recent ZOE Conference in Nashville, Tennessee;

> The first time I remember reading of such a distinction was in McLaren's *Finding Faith* and *it rocked my world then and it still does.* [emphasis mine, RM] Probably because I come from a Christian tradition that emphasized right belief about "salvation issues" in such a stark way. [215]

The "distinction" that Wade Hodges refers to here refers to a partial review he did on his blog on a book called ***How (Not) to Speak of God*** by Peter Rollins. Hodges says this, defining "distinction," . . . should exchange [my words RM]

---

[215]   See wadehodges.com. Blog posted on 10.11.06 @ 10:13 a.m. The Posting is entitled "How (Not) to Speak of God." Emphasis mine (RM)

... the Greek influenced idea of orthodoxy as right belief ... and rediscover the more Hebraic and mystical notion of the orthodox Christianity ... [216]

Translation:

(1) "Orthodox" to the emergent is synonymous with Eastern Mysticism. The term "Orthodox" is far different to the faithful than it is to the emergent who says that "orthodoxy" has NOTHING to do with "rightly dividing the word of truth."

(2) This "distinction" is part of what has been termed among us as the "new hermeneutic." [Note that to which Hodges refers as "Greek" is *linear* and "Hebraic, mystical & Orthodox" are *circular* as previously covered.]

Secondly, and even more telling, are the very scary sentiments of Greg Taylor;

---

[216] Ibid.

Brian McLaren is a great Christian leader and thinker of our time. *New Wineskins* has reviewed his writing, I've interviewed him, and asked him both to speak at our ZOE Leadership Conference and write for the magazine. In the most recent *New Wineskins* piece, "An open letter to Worship Songwriters," McLaren set forth a bold vision and challenge for worshippers to write songs that embody ancient truths and speak to emerging culture today. [217]

Remember, this is the same Brian McLaren that believes that "Muslims, Budhists and Hindus" may come into the kingdom before Christians will, that salvation means "saving the planet" and the kingdom is nothing more than a buffet of various social causes. It bears repeating, McLaren is not like you and I. He has such a low esteem for Scripture as to make one wonder why he ever even bothers darkening the door of any church building:

But my mission isn't to figure out who is already blessed [saved-RM], or not blessed, or un-blessable. My calling

[217] See gregtaylor.cc. Posting of 05.02.05 entitled; "Wineskins Devotional @ Pepperdine Wednesday," posted by Greg under "General."

is to be blessed so I can bless everyone. I'm going to Los Angeles! [In lieu of going to heaven—RM]

Recently I received an e-mail saying, "I heard a rumor that you're a universalist. Is that true?" Since I don't offer my exclusivist [those who believe that some people will go to heaven but most will not-RM] friends their expected answer to "the hell question," I can see why this rumor would spread. Rumors like this make me want to be an exclusivist who believes that only universalists go to heaven—after all, they have the highest opinion possible about the efficacy and scope of the saving work of Jesus! Or else I could be an inclusivist [universalist—RM] who believes that all but exclusivists are going to heaven. But no, that's ridiculous. Anyway, I'm going to Los Angeles. The old universalism pronounces that the Good News was efficacious for all individual sold AFTER [emphasis Brian McLaren] death, in heaven, beyond history. Inclusivism says the gospel is efficacious for many, and exclusivists say for a comparative few. But I'm more interested in a gospel that is universally efficacious for the whole earth BEFORE [emphasis Brian McLaren] death in history. [218]

Despite the fact that McLaren is not a Christian, in the New Testament sense of the term, his vision of "Christianity" has been embraced by some of the most influential people, congregations and organizations once among us. If you think I exaggerate, on October 26, 2005, Brian McLaren spoke to the student body during chapel at Pepperdine University. You can hear and see Brian McLaren set forth his theology for yourself by visiting the Pepperdine website to see and hear for yourself. Without micro analyzing the content, there is much philosophizing and precious little Scripture. It appears, therefore, to this writer that McLaren is much more of a philosopher than he is a theologian. [219]

Though many would call McLaren a "heretic," such a characterization is incorrect. In order to be a heretic, one must have first of all been a Christian at some point in time. McLaren, to my knowledge is not or has ever been, a Christian, in the New

[218]   Brian McLaren, *op. cit.,* pg. 113-114
[219]   From www.pepperdine.edu/Site Index/"A-Z"/Choose "S"/"Student Activites"/"Convocation-Chapel"/"Convo-Chapel Video Archieves"/"Previous Videos"/"Fall 2005"/"Brian McLaren"]

Testament since of the word. Think about it, a total outsider has more influence among "some" among us than any faithful Christian, alive or dead! I have said this once already and now must say it again:

Brian McLaren does not believe in a literal heaven and hell where the obedient are saved and the disobedient are damned. He rejects the fact that the Scriptures contain the linearly clear, totally inerrant and 100% inspired Word of God! Brian McLaren believes in the "here and now" and could not care less about the "here after." Now here this: Brian McLaren and his cabal are injecting this error into the church of Christ and want to bring it to YOUR congregation! [220]

No non-Christian has held such sway among Christians since Constantine officiated over church councils BEFORE his own baptism in the fourth century, ushering in the first great apostasy of the Dark Ages.

One closing thought here. After embracing *deconstructionist* Brian McLaren and his teachings, Hodges and Taylor have now co-authored an article appearing in the Winter 2007 issue of

---

[220] See Chapter 8 of this book for the original context of these comments.

Leadership Journal entitled "We Can't Do Megachurch Any More." In the article, Hodges and Taylor refer to the church of Christ as *"our denomination."* [emphasis mine, RM] Underscoring the point, the article was endorsed and linked on the main page of the ever more emergent leaning evangelical mouthpiece *christianitytoday. com* on February 1, 2007. Apparently all this was just a warm up for bro. Taylor's March-April 2008 "new 21st century restoration" article we have already discussed.

The Emergents among us are, in fact, highly organized. Though not "claiming" to be a "movement," there are several major emergent conferences each year, the "ZOE Conference" in Nashville, Tennessee, regional ZOE Conferences around the country such as Lubbock, Texas in March, 2007, the aforementioned "Tulsa International Soul Winning Workshop" in Tulsa Oklahoma and various and sundry meetings at Rochester College in Michigan. Rochester College was once a faithful Christian college known as Michigan Christian College. Rochester *"appears"* now to be, top to bottom, totally emergent and is now the "intellectual" center of the emergents among us. One can now add the annual ACU Lectureship since the recent public embrace of the self denominated "Christian Church" by the president of that once stalwart institution. Several leading Emergents are products of ACU. Sadly, Brian McLaren was a prominent speaker for the September, 2008 "Summit" Lectureship at ACU. As I have continually stated, please don't take my word for it, check it out for yourself! ACU, without blush or embarrassment, endorses without disclaimer (by direct linkage): the ZOE Group ®, the OOZE Community ® and the Worship Ministry of the Willow Creek Association ®, among other Emergent organizations. [221]

Sadly, we must now add Lipscomb University in Nashville to the growing list of Emergent activist entities among churches of Christ that are embracing Brian McLaren *et al.* Forty years ago, the Beatles ® sang these words; "The magical mystery tour is waiting to take you away, waiting to take you away."[222] In October, 2008 Lipscomb University put on a "theological expression of mystery and *imagination"*—not for band students—but for gospel preachers! Unlike similar programs in the past where the agenda was hidden "between the lines," this gathering proudly announces its agenda beginning with its title:

---

[221]   See: http://www.acu.edu/campusoffices/chapel/resources/links.html

[222]   Lyrics courtesy: www.sing365.com

"Reclaiming the Imagination: The Exodus as Paradigmatic Narrative for Preaching"[223]

Let's examine the stated purpose of the university for this conference as it appears on their website. In order to better understand the very circular, deliberate, muddled and political campaign quality word-smithing, I have made commentary by number whenever real, objective and definitional English is required for understanding:

"This conference ["Reclaiming the Imagination (1): the Exodus as Paradigmatic (2) Narrative (3) for Preaching"] proposes that we allow (4) the worlds (5) imagined (1) in the essential biblical narratives (6) to dramatically shape our preaching and lives. We believe that preaching reconstitutes (7) biblical paradigms (2) when it engages Scripture's vision by representing (8) what is absent (9) and making present what is inaccessible (10) to the end that followers of God will live into (11) a God-shaped reality (12)."

(1) "Imagination" is a concept from the 13th century theories of Thomas Aquinas. Aquinas taught, as did Aristotle before him,

---

[223]   See: http://preaching.lipscomb.edu/default.asp?SID=205

that truth comes primarily from our "senses," one of which . . . according to the musings of Aquinas . . . is "imagination." In other words, "if" you can "imagine" truth . . . it becomes truth, at least to you. Aquinas' teaching is a pillar of Roman Catholicism which HEAVILY relies on the "images" of mystery, art, music, sculpture, drama, etc. as does the "emerging" church of Brian McLaren *et al.*

(2) The word "paradigm" is a word that has little, if any, inherent definition since people who like to use it do so for the purpose of being able to "pour in their own "meaning." Perhaps more than any other, "paradigm" is the quintessential Post-Modern word . . . a poster child for the celebration of contradiction and confusion. The word calls for constant and never ceasing change. What is right today is wrong tomorrow. Today's sufficiency is deficient tomorrow. In business it is articulated by the phrase "continuous improvement." Using such a theory one never reaches the truth, for truth is an illusion to those who embrace the "paradigm." Here, in part, is what the ***BBC Edited Guide Entry*** has to say about this word:

> . . . the word paradigm had its origin as an obscure bit of linguist jargon. It derives from the Greek verb *deiknumi*, 'pointing out or exhibiting something', and the preposition

para, 'side by side', which then becomes *para-deigma*, a pattern, model or example . . . Thomas Kuhn was trained as a 20th-century physicist. One day, while preparing for his doctoral dissertation, he attempted to read Aristotle's *Physics*, the most influential work in the field of physics until Newton. Kuhn found that despite his extensive schooling in physics, he was completely unable to understand anything Aristotle was saying—in fact, it sounded like nonsense. [224]

As crazy as it sounds, Kuhn then began applying the subjectivity and constant change of Aristotelian philosophy, first to physics and then to business. This is why when you attend a company business meeting and the presenter begins to speak about a "paradigm shift," you know that the "old paradigm" didn't work and now a "new paradigm" is needed! By implication, therefore, when the planners of this conference chose this word "paradigmatic," it is a stealth way of saying that the way we have preached Exodus up until now [singular person and inspired writer, Moses who was transfigured with Christ, wrote the Book of Exodus that is, therefore, inerrant, full of truth and contains no error whatsoever] is no longer useful or valid. In other words, we need a "new paradigm," one that embraces

---

[224] See: http://www.bbc.co.uk/dna/h2g2/A2280674

the "story"/"narrative" and ignores the "details," which are simply "legendary" and not "verifiable." By using this word in the title of the conference, the sponsor(s) are clearly stating that there is no ultimate truth discoverable about the Book of Exodus and therefore no objective truth to be found in the study or the application of it. Should you think my analysis is too far "out there," keep in mind that one of the speakers at the conference is bro. Mark Hamilton of ACU who publicly contends that Moses did not actually write the Pentateuch, it was instead "compiled" from various "writers" in the 7th century B.C.! "IF" Moses did not write the Pentateuch, why in the world did Jesus Christ say that Moses "wrote of me?" Taken to its rational [I am assuming here that you, dear reader, are rational!] conclusion, "if" Moses did not write of Jesus Christ, would it not render Jesus Christ just another well-meaning, but deluded, religious leader . . . and turn our faith in a perfect savior into so much theological dust?

(3) The word "narrative" is a post-modern word substitute for "story." "Story" has been pragmatically substituted with "narrative" for the word "story" carries with it a FICTIONAL predisposition. McLaren believes that the Scriptures are primarily and foremost a "collection" of "smaller stories," many of which are little more than

legend and folk-lore. These "stories," not to be taken literally, lead us the "greater truth of the whole."

(4) "Allow?" Who is in charge here, God or man?

(5) The use of the plural "world(s)" is an illusionary way to say that there are "multiple meanings" for Scripture and that God has "multiple wills." This is all via the allegorical interpretive method of Origen whose speculations form, along with those of Aquinas, the foundational presuppositions for this conference.

(6) By heavy implication, since there are "essential biblical narratives," then there propositionally must be "NON-essential biblical narratives!" Pray tell, Mr. McLaren, which is which and how would we possibly know?"

(7) "Reconstitutes" (". . . to restore to a former condition by adding water.")[225] is another post-modern pragmatically chosen substitute word to hide the Satanic delusions of "deconstructionim and reconstructionism" taught by agnostic theologian Derrida *et al.* In other words, we must "deconstruct" the "flawed paradigm" of

---

[225]   Webster's Ninth New Collegiate Dictionary, (Merriam-Webster, Inc. 1991), pg. 984

preaching that Exodus is REVELATION and "reconstruct" a "new paradigm" that Exodus is NARRATIVE, a "story," a "fable" and a "compilation" of the "legends" of flawed and "evolving" humans . . . humans that were far less sophisticated than these attending "scholars" with thousands of years of "tradition" and "experience" unknown to the ancients at their whim and disposal.

(8) The word "representing" is an all-telling one. The Scripture, especially Exodus, is NOT written in obscure, clouded and allegorical style! Exodus is HISTORY, real history. However, McLaren and his confederates would have us all believe that Exodus is more akin to apocrypha! Any 1st semester freshman taking Intro to the Old Testament would know the difference between history and metaphor. This is just another example of the fetish that the "higher criticism" school has with symbolism, not only symbolism but personally defined symbolism at that! We, if we buy into this mystic and neo-Gnostic babble, get to make up our own individually defined symbolic "meanings!" [bro. Origen, you should have never listened to bro. Clement. bro. Clement, you should have never listened to Philo. And, Philo, YOU should have never listened to Plato!] By making the clear, linear and unambiguous Word of God mean something entirely different from its original and singular

meaning . . . all of a sudden we, in our own foolish and "darkened minds" are off the "sin hook!" [NOT!]

(9) Origen and his subsequent Roman theologians taught, as does the "fuller sense" (*sensus plenoir*) theory, that Scripture contains "hidden messages" and that these "hidden messages" are mystically revealed to modern day readers by the Holy Spirit. In other words, McLaren, LaRue, Dewey, York, Hamilton and Taylor "may" have access to "truths" that somehow have eluded all men in history (including the inspired writers themselves!) until this "imagination tour." One more salient point: these "hidden messages" and "multiple meanings" of Origen constitutes one of the pillars of Roman Catholicism according to Benedict XVI as he articulated on April 27, 2007, as noted earlier in this book.

(10) In line with the previous point, it is heavily implied by the phrase "making present what is inaccessible," that there is "truth" that has somehow been unobtainable until now. And now, Brian McLaren and his fellow presenters are going to bring us these "truths?" The phrase "making present what is inaccessible" is contradictory in the Kierkegaard mold, celebrating confusion as "truth." How can something that is "present" be at the same

time "inaccessible?" It cannot. Such a statement replicates the manic-depressive madness of Kierkegaard that he embraced as philosophy . . . a philosophy celebrated by the purpose of this conference.

(11) "Into" is a substitute word for "emerge" which is stealthily avoided by whoever wrote this introductory paragraph.

(12) "A (note the author uses "A" instead of "The") God-shaped reality" strongly suggests that God does not have a singular will but instead distributes . . . cafeteria style . . . "multiple realities," all equally valuable and obtainable by random choice. To take this line of thinking to its logical conclusion, then the "Christian reality" is just as valid as the "Muslim reality" and the "Hindu realty" and the "Save-The-Planet-From-Evil-Capitalism reality."

The word obfuscation in this introduction is staggering, so much so that Brian McLaren may have just written it himself! "The magical (imagination) tour is waiting to take you away!" What would Peter, John and Jude have to say? Friends, they (by the direct inspiration of the Holy Spirit) ALREADY said it in I Peter, II Peter, I John, II John, III John and Jude!

As with many conferences today, the "Preachers Conference" at Lipscomb serves as a "reunion" of sorts for Emergents. Not only do they like congregating together, they like writing together under the same roof. The Emergents among us "appear" to favor publishing under the name of LeafWood Publishers, now merged with the once venerable ACU Press. [226] Many LeafWood authors are found on the ZOE and *New Wineskins* websites and are regulars on the marquees of both the "ZOE Conference" and the "Tulsa Workshop" as well, not to mention the ACU Lectureship, Lipscomb confrences and others. The Emergents are zealous, organized, financed and focused on "coming soon to a congregation near you." They are primarily influenced by the errors of Origen and Aquinas, enamored with Evangelicalism and blindly propelled by Post-Modernism.

It is my prayer, sincerely repeated each time I take to my computer, that this work . . . God willing . . . shall bring repentance to the ranks of all Emergents in the church of Christ.

---

[226]   See leafwoodpublishers.com/aboutus

16. An Emergent Doctrinal Statement Examined

This work closes with a close examination of a doctrinal statement from an Emergent church in Charlotte, NC. Nothing clarifies matters more than the written word. Here is what Emergent Theology looks like when the Jello ® finally gets nailed to the wall!

People who once considered themselves part of the church of Christ and are now part of "emergent churches" have a "belief system" that is difficult to describe in objective detail as their outlook is, for the most part, subjective and Post Modern. When boiled down to the core, the Emergent church emphasizes two major departures from biblical example. The Emergents have created both a new leadership and a new worship "reality." Their theology in these two areas bears little resemblance to biblical, revealed truth and the New Testament congregational leadership and worship models. We will look at leadership first followed by worship. As stated previously, I will rely on the Kinetic Christian Church for much of this material since they have published a manifesto-type document on their web site that clearly articulates where they stand on these issues. [227] Keep in mind that since Emergent churches are Post Modern to their very core, no two are entirely alike. There are, however, similarities. I continue to urge you not to take my word for any of this but to examine the web sites of these theologically emergent churches and blogs for yourselves in the light of God's Word. I will cover these two departures of leadership and worship using a question and answer format. The question is phrased in my own words, the answers are direct quotes from the Kinetic Christian Church Launch Plan.[228]

Leadership

1. What is the purpose of the Kinetic Christian Church (KCC)? *". . . (to) guide people on their journey to know and imitate God."*

2. How does the KCC view the relationship of Christ with non-Christians? *". . . we desire to eliminate barriers between Christ and the un-saved."*

---

[227] "Kinetic Christian Church Launch Plan," a PDF downloadable file on the KCC website, kineticchurch.com (I encourage you to download the PDF and read it for yourself though the Post Modern way of speaking renders much of it obtuse. [RM]) NOTE: This material "may" no longer be posted

[228] Ibid

3. How would you describe the makeup of the KCC? *"KCC is a multigenerational church that targets young marrieds and singles between the ages of 24-35."*

4. How does KCC leadership plan to keep visitors coming back? *". . . visitors will be drawn back and will make the new church their church home through practical and relevant messages, culturally relevant services (including music, dramas & video), a safe seeker sensitive environment, a strong children's ministry, experiencing first hand the warmth and love, a large selection of life changing small groups . . ."*

5. How does the KCC leadership view the Bible? *"(The) Bible is truth without any mixture of error."*

6. What six positions make up the KCC leadership team? *"Leader Minister, Creative Director, Worship Leader, Children's Minister, Coach and Mentor."*

7. Does man have "good" in him? *"Although man has tremendous potential for good, he is marred by an attitude of disobedience toward God called "sin."*

8. How is the KCC organized? (NOTE: on the PDF download there is a triangular shaped drawing depicting as to how the church is organized with the phrase; "Basic Beliefs" at its base. The chart, sadly, does not contain a single reference to Christ, to God or to the scripture.) *"Basic beliefs, purpose, core values, vision, summary, behaviors, program & staff."* (NOTE: At the top of the triangle diagram is a green dot. What or who that represents is not made clear.)

9. Does the KCC have deacons? Deacons are neither named or described in the document, apparently the KCC does not have deacons.

10. Who has overall leadership responsibility at the KCC? *"Our senior minister will have overall leadership responsibility over all ministries. Our staff will have leadership responsibilities over everything within their assigned areas of responsibilities."*

11. Does the KCC have an eldership? *"Our management team will provide general oversight and counseling (serving essentially as elders for the new church.")* NOTE: Who is actually ON the mgt. team is not detailed. No mention is made as to the qualifications of these individuals. Furthermore, no one is named or identified on the web site as an "elder."

12. Is participation in small groups required of the KCC membership? *"One of the requirements and expectations for membership is small group involvement. This third tier of the assimilation strategy is key to promoting spiritual health and growth of each church member through relational progression. Groups will meet at least twice a month and will include, but are not limited to: Bible study, community & prayer."* (NOTE: As to exactly what "relational progression" is and just how "community" is defined, we do not know.)

Worship

1. What are the "sacred sacraments" of the KCC? *"Scripture reading, prayer, weekly communion, offering & baptism."*

2. Can you describe a worship service at KCC? *"Our worship and children's programming is multi sensory and encourages it's participants to respond. We use the city's best musicians, artists, actors, singers and dancers."*

3. What is a typical worship hour like? *"Our typical weekend gathering will include high impact worship and a 23 minute relevant message."*

4. Can you be more specific? *"We have a creative, age-appropriate ministry, that includes music, drama, activities, small groups and a lesson from the Bible. Our children's ministry is for infants through 6th grade and it meets concurrently with each adult service . . . . Junior and senior high students connect with the young high energy worship experience that the adults enjoy and are encouraged to attend with the adults . . . Kinetic's view of music is that it fits within the grander scope of the fine arts (music, drama, dance, traditional and electronic media). It's our belief that churches worldwide have forgotten that at one time, the church was the place to go to see the arts expressed as glory to God. Whether it was sculpture, music, stained*

glass, woodcarving or painting—the church had the corner on it. And the result was that people were drawn to God through the use of it. It is our intention to take back the arts for the glory of God. That is why you will see all the fine arts variously used in our services."

CONCLUSION

Those *Emerging Towards Apostasy*, are doing so by embracing Post-Modern philosophy, by becoming unequally yoked with denominational Evangelicalism and by the adoption of a Patristic and neo-Gnostic interpretive method based upon the teachings of Origen and Thomas Aquinas personified by the philosophy of Brian McLaren and his confederates.

I have attempted to define the terms, to identify the participants and to reveal the practices of the "theologically Emergent" among us. We now can clearly see what drives the Emergent church to its erroneous conclusions:

- An open embrace of Post-Modern thought and practice.

- An un-equal yoking with the Evangelical movement driven by men like Alan Jones and Brian McLaren who openly reject the inerrant Word of God on nearly every level.

- The full fledged adoption of a neo-Gnostic and narcissistic interpretive model based upon the false teachings of Origen and Thomas Aquinas, the same theological foundation on which Roman Catholicism was built.

May God grant the wavering "pre-Emergents" new courage to abandon their intentions to surrender conviction. May God grant both the "Emergents" and the "post Emergents" the discovery of a truth guided way back home to the faithful church, the body of Christ. May God grant to the faithful renewed courage & conviction to stay faithful. There is great potential harm to the Lord's church if we do not act to protect and educate all of our people in the Word . . . and how to "rightly divide it."

I have concluded that before it was possible for our erring brethren to "emerge," be swayed by Post-Modernism or become enamored by Evangelicalism that the love, study and correct understanding and interpretation of the Scriptures became a thing of the past. And, just what does "correct understanding and interpretation of the Scriptures" mean? Simply this: *The Scriptures Mean What They Say and Say What They Mean!* It is the assertion of this writer that God did not give us a Message that was clouded, befuddled, hidden and obscure *UNLESS* we insist on making it so by forcing our own pre-conceived notions onto the Sacred Text! God's Word, approached

BY FAITH is clear, unambiguous and understandable! Falsehood cannot prevail when the Scriptures are cherished and "meditated upon day and night" by the people of God. Only when the love and · the study of the Word goes into decline does Satan have an open door. The door swung wide open by our collective neglect (God forgive us!) and he and his surrogates walked right in and sat down on the podiums of our worship places, as it were.

Therefore, the *root* of all this trouble is the sad truth that some among us have adopted a neo-Gnostic Patristic interpretive model to understand and teach Scripture. These methods deny the singular original meaning of the text and instead force multiple *imaginary* "meanings" onto the Holy Word, changing it entirely. Right becomes wrong, light becomes dark, good becomes evil (see Isaiah 5:20), singing "to one another" becomes a rock and roll band and Sunday becomes Saturday. God no longer "gave His only begotten Son," He is instead, in the eyes of the Emergent guru Brian McLaren, some kind of spiritual child abuser from the far reaches of the universe. Our own bro. Greg Taylor no longer is compelled to share the Gospel with un-immersed Anglicans and teaches his children that there is little difference between the church of Christ and Methodism. Bro. Lucado has embraced the National Association of Evangelicals to the point of leadership. The list of spiritual surrenders grows longer with each passing week.

When I began this work in 2006, I thought that a sincere desire to reach the Post-Modern world had compelled many among us to embrace Emergent Theology. I now sadly know that Post Modernism is simply a convenient vehicle with which to transport the interpretive teachings of Origen and Thomas Aquinas, the very same interpretive model embraced by Romanism for some 1,000 + years. Such a model, if adopted, will lead us where it led Romanism . . . to APOSTASY. Our Lord and Savior Jesus Christ tells us that "the way is narrow and FEW there are that find it" (Matthew 7:14). Alan Jones, Brian McLaren *et al* say otherwise. This writer, and I pray you will as well, is sticking to Jesus Christ!

We know that Satan is the "father of lies and is a liar from the beginning." He told Eve in the garden that she "would NOT surely die." Sadly, both she and her husband proceeded to die for that very lie! In the end result, Emergent Theology will claim "salvation" for nearly everyone . . . Christian, Jew, Muslim, Hindu, Pagan, Scientologist, etc. This is Satan's great lie of spiritual deception. You see, my friend, Satan was the first Post-Modernist, the first

Evangelical, the first Emergent and will be the very first to greet the deceived masses at the gates of hell. I speak these words, not in judgment, but in tearful warning for "knowing the terror of the Lord," I am trying to persuade you my erring Emergent brother and sister. TURN BACK, while there is still time!

That being said, just for "arguments sake" let's "assume" for a moment that there is nothing biblically wrong with anything that the "theologically Emergent" are doing and saying. EVEN SO, their actions, done in relative secrecy up until the summer of 2006 have "sown discord among the brethren," a thing that God hates. (Proverbs 6:19) Not only that, the actions of the "theologically Emergent" CLEARY violate the principles of Romans 14 which teach that we should refrain from any practice that purposely harms the unity of the body. *Christianity is characterized by the rights we give up, not by the rights we assert.* Contemplate the seriousness of just what is at stake by prayerfully re-reading Ezekiel 3:16-21. We are all God's watchmen.

One would assume by reading the **Christian Chronicle** news accounts in the summer of 2006 that all of this is "just over the instrument." However, the instrument is just the "tip of the iceberg."

In reality, the issue over the instrument is a straw man in comparison with the theological interpretive errors that were embraced to make the instrument possible! We have crossed into new territory. In our past, those who have chosen the way of digression have at least "attempted" to defend their views with scripture. Not so in our day! If you remember nothing else, post—modern Emergent theologians *rarely* refer to the Holy Word to justify their beliefs and actions, they appeal to their own intellect, reason and emotions to define who they are and what they "believe," however we know "that the way of man is not in himself: it is not in man that walketh to direct his steps." (Jeremiah 10:23)

No, my friends, these events are not simply over the use of the instrument. As unbiblical as *THAT* idea is, these events are about *deconstructing* the church of Christ and *reconstructing* an entirely new and different church . . . one that is not of us; ". . . for if they had been of us, they would no doubt have continued with us: but they went out, that they might be made manifest that they were not all of us." (I John 2:19b)

You may ask; "What can I do about this?" It is really quite simple.

First of all, pray for wisdom as you approach those who are wayward.

Secondly, if you know of individuals or congregations that are emergent or sliding in that direction, please give them a copy of this book and initiate a dialogue and Bible study with them regarding these matters.

Go to them in private first as Jesus instructed us in Matthew 18.

If necessary as follow up, go finally to the elders with your witnesses if no heed is given to your love of souls.

Encourage the elders in your congregation to initiate Bible teaching on matters of salvation, worship, leadership, congregational autonomy and proper interpretation of the Scriptures.

Urgently pray for all the souls involved especially those *Emerging Towards Apostasy.*

Do all things with gentleness and respect noting full well Paul's instructions to "live peaceably with all men as much as it depends upon you." (Romans 12:18 Paraphrase)

May God bless the faithful and give time to the apostate!

APPENDIX #1
A SHORT HISTORY OF PHILOSOPHY IN WESTERN CIVILIZATION

By: J. T. Wheeler, Charlotte, NC

Having to chart the history of philosophy is a daunting task. At its best, it will come across as piecemeal and simplistic. Nevertheless, a picture of the scope of men's ideas affecting us today is necessary if we are to get some perspective on the forces shaping our culture and even our own individual efforts day-to-day.

Though Plato is seen as the premiere western philosopher, it is Protagoras, the father of humanism, who has "set the sail" of men's thoughts. "Man is the measure of all things" repeatedly shows up in discussions after him, either in word or substance of thought.

As we pass the Epicureans ("Let us eat and drink, for tomorrow we die"), their motto sounds too familiar to today's feel-good culture to ignore. We bow to the great benefit of Christianity, that supernatural display of "the treasure of all wisdom and knowledge" summed up in Christ Jesus, according to His New Testament. We are then

281

confronted with the ancient Gnostics, who sought to appropriate Christianity to their own ends.

In the Christian age, two lines of thought take hold: the common sense, linear view of Scripture, and therefore this view for the nature it explains, and the allegorical view, where men's thoughts ran free with less and less consideration to the boundaries the Scriptures provide. Augustine is the prime thinker here for the next thousand years, until Martin Luther shakes the world with his efforts of Sola Scriptura (*Scripture Alone*).

From Luther's efforts of understanding which exulted in free will and the equality of all men before God, three base branches of bitter fruit applied that thinking to a perversity of belief that embraced man without God, again the monster humanism rearing its heads for more victims. The first would be rank philosophy of thought which showed itself in Thomas Hobbes, then David Hume, and then Payne, and Twain, and finally in Bertrand Russell. The next would be the "sciences" of thought which, again building on Hobbes, branched further into various disciplines by the pen of John Stuart Mill, Darwin, Marx, Freud, Sanger, then finally Kinsey. Lastly, we glance at the inroads of such thinking into the religious disciplines.

Jefferson is notable here, then Wellhausen, Bultmann's so-called neo-orthodoxy, and finally it concludes with Altizer's "God Is Dead" mantra.

Thus from these three bitter branches filled with the seeds of bad ideas, we today are bombarded with militant atheism, having barely survived the harvest of such in the last century (Nazism, Communism). Immorality is rampant, families disintegrate, crime escalates, and the youth are destroyed, as any reason to hope is ripped away from them, except in what feeble offers are made by an ever-expanding central government.

Into this quagmire of surrender comes the Emergent Church, determined to rationalize and make respectable an atheistic approach to Scripture, allowing from it only what will expand the pride and power of the self-loving sinner. How to interpret and understand the Bible is for them to create, even as they are determined to allow nothing from that Book that might upset them.

How different from the early Christians and their efforts to know God, so that they might serve Him only and please Him in all things! How different from the mentality of the wonderful Lucian of Antioch and his efforts to see in the Scripture only what was plainly there! The idea of linear reasoning with its logic, attention to grammar, and understanding of context has made the Bible understandable through all these centuries, when others would hide the truth by their own darkened imagination.

Jesus Himself reveals the key to understanding God's holy word, as well as what place it should hold in our mind and lives. Though we might be separated by centuries from the original penmen and their paper, still Direct Command is to command us (Matthew 15:3-9). Approved Example guided the early church as it is to guide us as well (Matthew 12:1-8). And Necessary Inference is necessary for proper understanding and teaching (Matthew 22:29-32). To follow Jesus is to recognize His example in studying God's word. And His example is valid and binding till He comes. To seek our own way here is to reject Christ, and therefore be rejected when He returns.

The trace of philosophical thought upon our culture is a study of light and darkness. What you choose to follow today may very well determine the future of that culture. And it will most certainly determine your own eternal destiny.

J. T. Wheeler

Charlotte, NC

NOTE: Bro. Wheeler preaches for the Mountain Island church of Christ in Charlotte, NC. His willingness to write this appendix is greatly appreciated!

APPENDIX #2

An Analysis of three theologically Emergent sermons preached at the Richland Hills church of Christ in Ft. Worth by Senior Minister Rick Atchley in support of the instrument and partaking of the Lord's Supper on Saturdays. Delivered in December, 2006:

These three sermons are lengthy and therefore present a challenge to decipher the material. As painful as it is to listen carefully to what Rick Atchely says, it is important to do so for these lessons are theologically Emergent from start to finish. These lessons possibly represent the best opportunity we have today to understand how Emergent theology really works when applied to a real life situation. As stated previously, PLEASE examine the Richland Hills website and weigh what is stated there against the weight of Scripture in a loving and kind Berean spirit. After so doing and after prayerful consideration, this writer concludes that the entire body of work must be rejected for the following reasons:

A. The entire concept is based solely upon a pragmatic and outcome based proposition of how Richland Hills could add another service without placing any inconvenience upon their current membership. There is no seeking of God's Will FIRST, only seeking the convenient and the practical. Only afterwards is any attention given to scripture, and then only in a circular fashion.

B. Despite the fact that Jude says that the "faith has been once forever deliverED (past tense) to the saints," that Peter says that God has "given (past tense) us ALL things pertaining to life and godliness" and that "God is (present tense) not a respecter of persons," Rick Atchley publicly and openly claims that the Holy Spirit personally told him to preach these sermons. "IF" the Holy Spirit, in fact, had spoken to Rick Atchley then we must ask this question, "Did God lie to Jude and Peter so He could then tell the truth to Rick Atchley?" And . . . by default, would that not mean that God "respects" Rick Atchley more that Jude and Peter?

C. In the long ago, Peter states that the "unlearned and unstable" will "wrest" (twist) scripture. Pounding round pegs into square holes, this "study" by bro. Atchley on instrumental music and communion wrests and twists numerous passages.

D. Clear apostolic and patristic history is either ignored or "reinterpreted" in a existential, superficial, subjective and Post-Modern way.

E. The church of Christ is continually spoken of in systematically un-kind language. The church for which Jesus died, the church Jesus promised to build is ignored and even potentially discarded by God according to Rick Atchley in his concluding remarks at the end of the 3rd lesson. Keep in mind that the central and core idea of Emergent theology is to DECONSTRUCT and then RECONSTRUCT the church. The purpose of the Emergents, in this writers view, is not to just simply add instruments and Saturday night communion, it is to completely change the church of Christ from the Blood Bought Body of Christ to just another denomination where one church is just as good as another.

For the sake of analysis, the above five reasons for rejection will serve as five categories in which I will place the various points and quotations from my notes taken from the on-line video sermons currently on the Richland Hills website. I apologize for any misquotations as I am not a professional transcriber. As far as I know, as of this writing, there are no transcribed copies of these lessons available for analysis. Should you, as you read this, know of one . . . please let me know.

As stated several times, these observations are not judgments, they are assessments. These observations do not go to motive, they go only to the facts of the matter.

It is my prayer that Rick Atchley, the eldership at Richland Hills and every person swayed by the "Both/And" sermons will renounce error and return to the love and faithfulness of our loving and gracious Savior.

This appendix "Interprets Scripture by Scripture." My comments will be one man's attempt to exegete these quotes, assertions and Scriptures in their proper context as well as to examine their logical conclusions. In order to reference the notes and/or quotations, the following format will be used:

EXAMPLE: 1-5:34] The first number represents either "Both/And" lesson 1, 2 or 3. The second two numbers represent the APPROXIMATE minute and second location in that sermon where the actual sound bite can be seen or heard on the RH website. Due to the audio and video formats used, it is difficult for the locations to be anything but general.) I will habitually refer to Rick Atchley as "RA." Finally, due to my limited technical resources, I lost track of the exact times during a large portion of "Both/And" Lesson 2 between 2-15: and 2-36:

A. The "Both/And" Lessons Are Pragmatically Conceived and Do Not First Seek God's Will Through His Word:

1-5:34—It is stated right up front that the driving force behind the decision to offer an instrumental service and communion on Saturday night was to allow the members to choose "which kind of service they wanted to attend and when."

1-8:01—It is stated in response to a "missional question"[229] in the form of rhetorical question; "Is it an effective strategy for this church at this time to have worship choices?"

1-8:54—Instead of citing scripture, Coach John Wooden is cited who said; "There is no progress without change."

---

[229] NOTE: See the discussion of the word "missional" toward the end of Chapter 8

1-16:34—It is stated that historically we have seen the debate between a cappella singing and instrumental music as an "either or" question. However, now, it is stated that it should be a "both/and" question.

1-19:20—It is stated that a cappella singing is o.k. "if that is your choice."

1-20:25—The term "preferred worship preference" is used.

1-36:25—In referring to the Jerusalem Conference of Acts 15, it is stated that the apostles and elders were more committed to the mission than to their heritage and that "they chose their mission over their tradition."

1-54:11—It is suggested that "if" we bring in the instrument then we will "stem the tide of gifted young leaders (who are leaving)."

2-34:46—It is suggested that "if" we bring in the instrument then we will no longer insult musicians. QUOTE: "Please do not say that you can only praise God from the heart with the voice and not the instrument. That is an unkind and an untrue insult to all believing musicians. Playing an instrument to the glory of God is not just an aid to worship, it is an act of worship . . . . Now many a cappella churches allow people with gifts in acting or in painting to bless the body. Why would we deny that same sweet privilege to our gifted musicians?"

[Authors note: "IF" this point is valid, what then will we do with electricians, salesmen, plumbers, brick layers and farmers *et. al.*? Will they too all be invited to "perform" their talents in worship? It goes without saying as well that acting and painting as acts of worship are also un-scriptural additions to our collective worship. There is no apostolic command, example or inference that any such activity EVER took place during the 1st century church of Christ. Such additions took place later as the Patristical influence took over.]

2-47:00—It is asserted (the documentation is elusive) that "thousands" have "studied the Bible INTO using the instrument and "none" have studied the Bible OUT of using the instrument.

[Authors note: Pragmatic decisions made to "attract" increasing numbers of people is not a biblical concept for Jesus said that the way to salvation is narrow and the way to destruction is broad. In addition, has RA not heard of the RESTORATION MOVEMENT where 100's of thousands studied their way, not only out of denominationalism, but out of the use of the instrument?! This seems to this writer as a complete and total denial of historical reality, a tell-tale trait of existentialism.]

2-50:23—QUOTE—"God does not segregate life to the point that what is acceptable in a car or in a wedding is not acceptable in a worship service." [Authors note: Since we all eat fast food in our cars, talk on our cell phones in our cars and carry on conversations in our cars, are these things also now acceptable in worship and as acts of worship?]

3-5:16—It is stated that Saturday evening at 5 p.m. is the least scheduled hour in America today, people are free to come to worship. The idea is to let the "tail wag the dog!"

3-5:59—It is stated that a Saturday evening "new" worship hour produces the least amount of change for those wanting to keep their existing time slots on Sunday morning.

3-6:19—It is stated that a Saturday evening "new" worship hour provides "more flexibility for future services."

3-11:22—QUOTE—"Choose the day (of worship) that is consistent with your conviction and your worship preference and your calling from God."

[AUTHORS NOTE: How would God call a person to do something that is not authorized in His Will?]

3-22:14—While speaking in regards to Saturday worship with communion it is stated that; "We will do it on Saturday and we will do it on Sunday."

3-22: 30—In order to justify worship on Saturday, it is asserted by Rick Atchley that; "I have never heard of a preacher having a problem taking up a collection on Saturday." [Authors note: In my entire life, I have never been to a Gospel Meeting or any other function among us where the preacher "asked for the plate to be passed." Have you? I truly do not know where this assertion comes from.]

3-26:47—QUOTE—"Follow your heart, your conviction and your conscience and worship where and when you choose without in any way judging a brother if he goes to another service."

[Authors comment: This quote reminds me of the old Debbie Boone song (Pat Boone's daughter) "How can it be wrong when it feels so right?"]

3-39:40—QUOTE—In regards to having an instrumental music worship service on Saturday where communion is served, it is stated; "Let's admit that all churches make cultural concessions to reach our neighbors . . . It is the culturally appropriate thing to do if we are going to bring our un-churched neighbors to worship with us."

3-41:28—QUOTE—"His truth has got to be clothed in time specific cultural forms. The ultimate expression of this is what we celebrate this time of the year (i.e. "Christmas"). Every year the arrival of Jesus as the Word become flesh, God entered our culture in a way we could understand. The incarnation calls on us to identify with lost people as Paul put it; "by all means possible." Now, in this culture I personally believe that this means instrumental music." . . . . "And what's happened in the last 30-40 years is that the young people have decided that we don't trust the people we are told to trust, the people that write the newspapers, that make the T.V. shows. They turn to the artists. Bob Dylan told the truth, John Lennon told the truth and this generation turned to music—hear this now (RA)—for their worldview. In this post-modern world they don't get their truth propositionally, they get it through experience and music is one of the preeminent ways they experience their world view. So they ask one question of music; "Does it lead me to your God or not?" And how many of this generation are listening to only a cappella music? How many of them have their buttons on their radios in their cars tuned to a cappella stations? How many of you do?"

3-46:11—QUOTE—"If our burden is to reach the lost, is our fellowship courageous enough to face the possibility, and I would say ever the probability, that our exclusive music preference hinders our evangelistic efforts?"

B. The "Both/And" Lessons Claim Extra-Biblical Latter Day Personal Revelation via The Holy Spirit Himself

2-3:23—It is stated that he (RA) knew 10 years ago he would have to preach this sermon whether or not Richland Hills would introduce an instrumental service.

2-3:52—RA recalls that the sermon that he preached 10 years ago was on Galatians 2 where Paul confronted Peter to his face for his hypocrisy.

2-5:30—QUOTE—"Right there in that spot about 1994 in the middle of my sermon, the Holy Spirit said to me (emphasis mine RM): "And that's what you and all the preachers like you are doing who haven't for years believed that the worship to God with instruments is wrong but you continue by your silence to let people think it's wrong to allow the body to be disrupted and you do so under the plea, "Well, we're maintaining peace," but that's not peace, that's cowardice." I knew then the day would come I'd have to teach this lesson."

[AUTHORS NOTE: "IF" the Holy Spirit "spoke" to RA 10 years prior to the quote, that would be *1996 not 1994*! What did the Holy Spirit "say" in 1996? RA neglects to relay *THAT* quote. The only Holy Spirit "quote" RA *DOES* give us is a quote from *1994*! 1994 would be *12 years in the past, not 10!* Now RA does say that it was "about 1994" but a *TWO YEAR VARIANCE* when the Holy Spirit speaks directly to you? Surely, the date and time would be remembered more precisely that a 2 year swing one way or the other. Another question; *WHO* did the speaking in 1994? Was it the Holy Spirit, or some other spirit? *The first two references do not match up with the quote!* Now we KNOW that God does not contradict Himself but RA's quotes DO!

Extra-biblical latter-day personal revelation is a contradiction with what God has ALREADY said and is therefore NOT possible.

The Scripture clearly states that "God IS (present tense meaning "now and forevermore" RM) no respecter of persons," (Acts 10:34) that "The faith was once deliver-*ED* (past tense RM) to the saints" (Jude 3) and that "His divine power hath giv-*EN* (past tense RM) to us ALL (emphasis mine RM) things pertaining to life and Godliness through the knowledge of Him that hath call-*ED* (past tense) us to glory and virtue." (II Peter 1:3)

C. The "Both/And" Lessons Consistently Take Scriptures Out of Context, "Pounding Round Pegs Into Square Holes"

Scriptures Regarding Instrumental Music:

1-20:15—It is stated that the "scriptural" basis for this entire theological re-mix is that RA has discovered a new understanding and application of the so-called "Jerusalem Conference" found in Acts chpt. 15. Let's look at the text in it's context and it's clear meaning. Recall as you consider the text that RA uses ALEXANDRIAN/CIRCULAR/SENUS PLENIOR interpretive methods that focus on multiple, obscure and hidden meanings that even the writers of scripture somehow "missed!"

> ACTS 15:1-32 "And certain men came down from Judea and taught the brethren, saying, Except ye be circumcised after the custom of Moses, ye cannot be saved. And when Paul and Barnabas had no small dissension and questioning with them, the brethren appointed that Paul and Barnabas, and certain other of them, should go up to Jerusalem unto the apostles and elders about this question. They therefore, being brought on their way by the church, passed through both Phoenicia and Samaria, declaring the conversion of the Gentiles: and they caused great joy unto all the brethren. And when they were come to Jerusalem, they were received

of the church and the apostles and the elders, and they rehearsed all things that God had done with them. But there rose up certain of the sect of the Pharisees who believed, saying, It is needful to circumcise them, and to charge them to keep the law of Moses. And the apostles and the elders were gathered together to consider of this matter. And when there had been much questioning, Peter rose up, and said unto them, Brethren, ye know that a good while ago God made choice among you, that by my mouth the Gentiles should hear the word of the gospel, and believe. And God, who knoweth the heart, bare them witness, giving them the Holy Spirit, even as he did unto us; and he made no distinction between us and them, cleansing their hearts by faith. Now therefore why make ye trial of God, that ye should put a yoke upon the neck of the disciples which neither our fathers nor we were able to bear? But we believe that we shall be saved through the grace of the Lord Jesus, in like manner as they. And all the multitude kept silence; and they hearkened unto Barnabas and Paul rehearsing what signs and wonders God had wrought among the Gentiles through them. And after they had held their peace, James answered, saying, Brethren, hearken unto me: Symeon hath rehearsed how first God visited the Gentiles, to take out of them a people for his name. And to this agree the words of the prophets; as it is written, After these things I will return, And I will build again the tabernacle of David, which is fallen; And I will build again the ruins thereof, And I will set it up: That the residue of men may seek after the Lord, And all the Gentiles, upon whom my name is called, Saith the Lord, who maketh these things known from of old. Wherefore my judgment is, that we trouble not them that from among the Gentiles turn to God; but that we write unto them, that they abstain from the pollutions of idols, and from fornication, and from what is strangled, and from blood. For Moses from generations of old hath in every city them that preach him, being read in the synagogues every sabbath. Then it seemed good to the apostles and the elders, with the whole church, to choose men out of their company, and send them to Antioch with Paul and Barnabas; namely, Judas called Barsabbas, and Silas, chief men among the brethren: and they wrote thus by them, The apostles and the elders, brethren, unto the brethren who are of the Gentiles in Antioch and Syria and Cilicia, greeting: Forasmuch as we have heard that certain who went out from us have troubled you with words, subverting your souls; to whom we gave no commandment; it seemed good unto us, having come to one accord, to choose out men and send them unto you with our beloved Barnabas and Paul, men that have hazarded their lives for the name of our Lord Jesus Christ. We have sent therefore Judas and Silas, who themselves also shall tell you the same things by word of mouth. For it seemed good to the Holy Spirit, and to us, to lay upon you no greater burden than these necessary things: that ye abstain from things sacrificed to idols, and from blood, and from things strangled, and from fornication; from which if ye keep yourselves, it shall be well with you. Fare ye well. So they, when they were dismissed, came down to Antioch; and having gathered the multitude together, they delivered the epistle. And when they had read it, they rejoiced for the consolation. And Judas and Silas, being themselves also prophets, exhorted the brethren with many words, and confirmed them."—1901 ASV

[AUTHORS NOTE: As we can see, there are numerous "points" in this passage to consider. RA, using his "circular" approach to the passage considers them all equally valid but not equal in importance. A minor point appears to have been made by him to be the ONLY point of the passage. This is consistent with what is called the "narrative" approach to scripture. Post modern theologians, especially Brian McLaren, consider the Bible to be just a narrative, a big panoramic story to give us the "big picture" (remember the *senus plenior* method) of God's intentions, details just don't really matter. This approach would be like someone asking directions to get from one specific address on the east side of town to another specific address on the west side of town and being told to "follow the setting sun as your conscience directs." In this case the "big picture" of this passage is simply, according to RA, that the apostles and elders chose to make these directives simply to make it easier for the Gentiles to come into the church. In other words, RA seems to want to create the apostles and elders intentions into his own pragmatic image. The "logic" goes like this (for discussions sake): "If the apostles and elders removed circumcision from the requirements of the faith so as to make it easier for the Gentiles to become Christians, then we can add instrumental music and change the worship hour from Sunday to Saturday in order to attract more people to the gospel." The "logic" is flawed in at least two ways; first of all the apostles and elders could not "remove" something from the gospel that was not there to start with. Secondly, as we see below, the conference was not called to discover ways to expand outreach to the Gentiles but to make sure that no one would be allowed to add to the gospel and then make the addition a condition of salvation. Flawed as it is, this same "logic" is being used in St. Louis as we speak. I am told that in order to attract more drinkers of alcohol to church, some denominations are now holding "services" in bars. Well . . . . "IF" RA is correct in this interpretation . . . . why not?!

Someone once put it this way; "Don't be so open minded so as to let your brain fall out of your head!" Circular interpretive methods are likewise so open minded as to let the truth fall completely out of a passage.

That's how RA seems to be interpreting this passage. Now, let's look at the passage and see what the PASSAGE says about the passage.

15:1-2—Certain men from Judea began to TEACH a different doctrine, adding circumcision to the gospel as a requirement for salvation. This action sets the stage for the entire passage. The passage is here, not because there was a "workshop" on how best to reach the Gentiles, but because "certain men from Judea" came down and added new conditions to God's plan of salvation. These teachers were attempting to do the unthinkable, dragging the dead carcass of a dead religion into the brand new and expanding church of Christ. They were, in effect, preaching "another gospel," about which Paul would later soundly condemn in his letter to the Galatians, chpt. 1, vs. 6-10.

15:2—This action did not bring Paul and Barnabas in to a theological conversation but "into sharp dispute and debate with them." (NIV) Despite what may have been the best of intentions, these brethren took sides against God's chosen apostle Paul. Now we know that Paul was sensitive to the cultural opinions of all men as we clearly see in Romans chpt. 14. That being the case, we KNOW that these matters were critical to the very essence of Christianity, not some opinion about outreach methodology, otherwise Paul and Barnabas would not have been in "sharp dispute and debate." These teachers apparently did not listen to what Paul and Barnabas had to say and exported their views southward to Jerusalem where they were taken up by some former Pharisees.

15:2—This debate, this dispute, became so heated as to prompt the elders in Antioch to send Paul and Barnabas to Jerusalem to speak to the apostles and elders at Jerusalem regarding this question. It was NOT a question regarding Gentile Outreach Methodology BUT it WAS a question as to whether or not requirements of the Old Law were to be added to the New Law as a prerequisite to salvation. To call upon the apostles was the ultimate appeal in that day and time. It was not entered into lightly for they spoke God's words!

15:4-5—The opposition was so determined in their error that while the church, the apostles and elders were welcoming Paul and Barnabas, the Pharisee sect stood up, interrupted the proceedings and demanded their views be heard by all! Error is not only divisive, it is brazen as well. Satan demands attention, even in the company of the apostles!

15:5—Error, then as now, is progressive. In Antioch, the opposition to Paul and Barnabas demanded only circumcision. Now in Jerusalem, they upped the ante to demand that Gentiles not only be circumcised, they demanded that they should keep the entire Law of Moses! Again, redundant as it may now be sounding to you as you read, there is NO MENTION by anyone of how to better evangelize the Gentiles and to make it "easier" for them to come into the church. The focus was in vs. 1 and still is in vs. 5 was that a sect was trying to add to the gospel by bringing back the Law of Moses and impose it upon the Gentiles as they became Christians.

15:6—When the assembly with the entire church became disrupted, the apostles and elders withdrew to discuss the issue. There was "much questioning" before any conclusions were drawn.

15:7-11—After this "much questioning," Peter got up and addressed the rest of the apostles and the elders.

He recalled that God Himself chose him (Peter) to share the gospel with the Gentiles. As a result, Peter was well qualified to speak on this matter.

He notes that God gave the Holy Spirit to the Gentiles just like He gave it to the Jews on Pentecost.

He notes that God shows no distinction between Jews and Gentiles.

He then boldly asserts that by requiring the keeping of the Law of Moses that they would literally be "putting God on trial."

He states that making the keeping of the law a requirement of salvation, they would set a standard that neither their ancestors or themselves were EVER able to bear!

He concludes his remarks by stating; "But we believe that we shall be saved by the grace of the Lord Jesus, in like manner as they." Dragging the dead carcass of the Law of Moses back across the saving grace of Jesus Christ is not only unnecessary, it would make said grace of no effect.

15:12—After Peter concluded his remarks, the apostles and elders fell silent as they listened to Paul and Barnabas relay all that God had done among the Gentiles WITHOUT the imposition of either circumcision or the keeping of the Law of Moses.

15:13-18—James, the brother in the flesh to Christ, arose and then by inspiration quotes a passage from Amos 9:11 and 12 that predicted that God would rebuild His Tabernacle including ALL the Gentiles that would call upon His Name. The "calling upon the Name of the Lord," was and is, to all Jews and Gentiles alike the simple act of Grace that we call baptism where sins are forgiven and the Gift of the Holy Spirit is given to the soul that is immersed. (Acts 22:16 and Acts 2:38) There is no distinction as to how Jews and Gentiles are added to the church of Christ.

15:19—James concludes (in the original language via *The Nestle Greek Text With a Literal English Translation* via Samuel Bagster and Sons Ltd. 1958 as included in Zondervan's 1970 edition of *The R.S.V. Interlinear Greek—English New Testament*): "Wherefore I decide not to trouble the [ones] from the nations turning to God . . ." Consistent with the text and the context, the word "trouble" means adding to God's will and forcing Gentiles to adhere to the Law of Moses as a condition of salvation. The aim here is not to "water down the gospel" but to PRESERVE the gospel and NOT to add to it!

There is absolutely no hint of pragmatic and outcome based speculative planning here on the part of the apostles and elders!

Unfortunately, this is the passage that RA "discovers" the hidden motivation of the conference, to make it "easier" for the Gentiles to enter the church.

[However, a BYPRODUCT of not binding the Law of Moses upon new Gentile believers would be "less troubling" according to James in Acts 15:19. We know that a "byproduct" of a thing is NOT the ESSENCE of a thing!]

RA "finds" that the apostles and elders did what they did in order to ramp up the numbers of Gentiles coming into the church. Such a "finding" is circular theology at it's very worst . . . finding something that is not even there to begin with. RA's conclusions are biblical interpretation by smoke and mirrors, in this writer's assessment. It is my hope and prayer that RA will reexamine the scriptures and return to the truth he once espoused and then re-teach this series "rightly dividing the Word of truth."

15:22—The apostles and elders then rejoined the church as a whole and decided to choose some of their own men and send a letter back to Antioch.

15:24—The letter details in this verse 4 things that these false teachers had done: (1) Certain men had gone out from the church at Jerusalem, (2) These men had "troubled . . . with words." (3) These men had "subverted their souls" and (4) These men went out without any authority to do so from the apostles and the elders. Consistent with the text and the context, the conclusion of the apostles and elders was that these "disturbers" had gone out to Antioch without permission or authority, that they had "troubled" and "subverted" souls with a message of adding to the gospel of Christ with a "requirement" for Gentiles to adhere to the Law of Moses in order to obtain salvation.

This passage concerns itself with the thwarting of any attempt to add to the gospel any provision not prescribed by Christ or His apostles. It is NOT a pragmatic approach to "outreach methodology."

15:25-26—The letter then reviews 4 things that Gentile Christians, worshipping together with Jews, were to continue doing: (1) Abstain from things sacrificed to idols; (2) to consume no blood; (3) to eat no meat of a strangled animal and (3) to abstain from fornication. Contextually, these simple practices would emphasize the fact that they were all "saved by the grace of the Lord Jesus" and that "works of law" were not only not necessary for salvation, they were to be totally cast aside!

It is shocking that RA would choose this passage on which to "hang" his entire argument upon! Not only does he completely miss the truth of the passage, he uses a passage of TOTAL OPPOSITION to Christian observance of the Law of Moses to argue FOR bringing in aspects of temple worship (instrumental music) and Sabbath keeping (Saturday night worship with communion) back into 21st Century

312

Christianity! Circular theology turns the scripture on it's head. It deconstructs (destroys) knowable truth and reconstructs (creates) "new" truth. This "new truth" somehow eluded the apostles, somehow eluded the elders at Jerusalem and somehow has eluded every person who ever studied the passage until either 1994 or 1996. Now, all of a sudden, this "new truth" comes to Rick Atchley and Rick Atchley alone when the Holy Spirit himself "reveals" all this "new truth" to him and to him alone!]

2-6:38 to 2-15:14

RA states that there are Old Testament "reasons" to add instrumental music (he calls music "praise") to Christian worship. He states that God did not only allow instrumental music in worship, He commanded it. That He did, no one disputes that. However . . . if we are to be true to RA's "logic" our church buildings would also have to be flowing with the blood of animal sacrifices along with every other Jewish custom and practice of that dead religion.

If you and I can go directly to the Old Testament for teachings on right living before God, I can have multiple wives, you can own slaves and our neighbor can divorce his wife with a "Post-It-Note!" ®

Discernment of these matters is what it means to "rightly divide the Word of Truth!" We must discern just who the primary recipient is, what dispensation they lived under and what is the context of the passage. Otherwise, we will truly be susceptible to "every wind of doctrine!"

Though he was in error on a great number of things, the late denominationalist Vernon McGee once observed, ". . . even though the Bible was written FOR each of us, it was not written TO each of us." For US, Hebrews interprets Leviticus, not the other way around! RA's logic would have us re-weaving the veil of the temple as it were.

Finally, should we look backwards to the law that could only "condemn" as opposed to looking to Christ who can truly SAVE us?! Instrumental music and Sabbath keeping belong in the Temple that Christ destroyed in 70 a.d. through Titus the Roman. We live in a much newer and better dispensation! Let's not go back to "works" when we have such "GRACE!"

II Chronicles 5:13-14: RA contends that since Solomon used instrumental music at the dedication of the Temple, so can we. [Why can't we use it in our worship? We CAN "IF" we add back ALL of the Law of Moses AND Rebuild AND Rededicate the temple.]

I Chronicles 28:18-19: David and David's seer(s) commanded instrumental music in worship, why can't we have it? [We CAN "IF" we add back ALL of the Law of Moses.]

Psalms 33:1-3: The psalmist used a harp, why not me? [I CAN "IF" I add back ALL of the Law of Moses.]

Psalms 92: 1-3: This is a Psalm SPECIFICALLY for the Sabbath day, NOT the Lord's Day!

Psalms 150:1-6: This, too, is nothing new. God DID command instrumental music in the Temple along with . . . . well, you fill in the blanks!

Psalms 81:1-5: This is a direct command of God "IF" you are the Chief Musician of the Family of Asaph! If you are not, this verse does not apply to you in a *literal* sense!

At this point RA makes a "point" that in essence states that "IF" we are "commanded" to "sing psalms, hymns and spiritual songs," then the very psalms we are commanded to sing, in turn "command" us to use the instrument! *The circular "logic" goes like this:*

1) God inspired the Psalms

2) God commands the use of the instrument in several Psalms

3) God commands that Christians sing Psalms

. . . therefore . . .

4) God commands (or at least allows) Christians
to use instruments in worship.

On the surface, it "seems" to make sense, doesn't it? Well, let's apply this "logic" to other Psalms:

Psalms 122:2—"IF" Christians are interpreting the Psalms so as to allow instrumental music in worship, then in order to be consistent, "our feet must stand within the gates of Jerusalem" as well.

Psalms 137:6—"IF" Christians are interpreting the Psalms so as to allow instrumental music in worship, then in order to be consistent, we must call a curse upon ourselves to cause "our tongue to cleave to the top of our mouth" if we do not esteem Jerusalem above all else.

Psalms 48:12—"IF" Christians are interpreting the Psalms so as to allow instrumental music in worship, then in order to be consistent, we must "walk around the towers of Zion" as well.

There are two points that I would like to make here. First of all, circular interpretation of SOME passages and NOT others causes one to become "double minded, unstable in all his ways." Secondly, if we pull any PART of the Law of Moses into the Christian Age, we MUST pull it all in . . . drag in the instrument . . . we'll have to have quite the barbeque (Kosher of course!) every day continually out in the parking lot!

We can, as Christians, read, study and sing Psalms containing references to Old Testament worship practices WITHOUT dragging those worship practices into the New Covenant.

God commanded the use of instruments in Temple worship, He has left no such instructions for us . . . there is NO contradiction! "IF" we insist on doing so, we would assume to add to the words of God regarding New Testament worship thus violating Proverbs 30: 6; "Add thou not to his words, lest he reprove thee, and thou be found a liar."

In this writers view, circular theology does just that, it adds to the Word of God by "finding" conclusions that are simply not there, much like modern day lawyers can "find" a "right to abortion" in the Constitution!

There is one other thing that strikes me odd about all of this. For years those who now find themselves among the emergent have accused the faithful church of taking scripture "out of context." NOW, it seems, that EVERY scripture that RA applies in this series does just that . . . takes each one "out of context." How ironic.

2-15:15—RA cites II Chronicles 5:13-14 to make this point; ". . . there is no hint that God was ever unpleased with instrumental music in the OT." And . . . ? Of course, God is pleased by that which He commands and then people faithfully follow! God COMMANDED the use of instrumental music in OT Temple worship, He has issued no such command for us today!

2-15: ?—Using Psalms 45:6-8, Hebrews 1:8-9 and Romans 15:8-9, RA appears to stretch interpretative methodology to beyond it's breaking point! He "claims" that these three passages teach "messianic prophesy that anticipates instrumental praise (in NT worship)." When referencing either the ASV, ESV, YLT or NIV, one finds in vs. 8 of Psalms 45; "Out of ivory palaces stringed instruments (emphasis mine RM) have made thee glad." (ASV) However, when referencing either the KJV1611, Webster, Douay Rheims 1899 and the KJV, we read; ". . . out of ivory palaces by which they have made thee glad." There is a clear division among OT scholars as to whether or not "stringed instruments" are even included in the passage . . . for better or for worse! EVEN MORE STRIKING, when these verses are quoted in Hebrews 1:8-9 AND Romans 15:8-9, they are quoted *WITHOUT ANY mention of "stringed instruments"* by ANY of the versions I checked!

However, just for arguments sake, lets "assume" for a moment that RA may be on to something regarding Psalms 45:6-8. Upon examination of the text, do we find a PAST TENSE VERB in reference to stringed instruments and God being pleased, or do we find a FUTURE TENSE VERB in reference to stringed instruments "pleasing God?" We find a PAST TENSE verb! A PAST TENSE verb would indicate that this praise would apply to only those singers in the . . . you guessed it . . . THE PAST! A FUTURE TENSE verb would "indicate" a use of instrumental music in NT worship! No such FUTURE verb appears!

Saying that these passages are some sort of "messianic prophesy that anticipates instrumental praise," is, perhaps, the most ambitious of RA's OT "proof text" defensive posture.

2-15:15fl.—RA references Psalms 81:1-5 and asserts again that the ". . . Holy Spirit commands us to sing Psalms we cannot practice" if instrumental music in NT worship is not allowed. [As mentioned before, ". . . all Scripture is written FOR us, but not all Scripture is written TO us." This passage CLEARLY was written TO those under the OT covenant! It is NOT written TO us today! Let the passage speak for itself:

"To the chief Musician upon Gittith, A Psalm of Asaph."—Psalm 81:1a

This passage is pulled out of context "IF" we apply it LITERALLY to us today. It was written TO the Temple musicians, players of instrumental music in OT worship which was commanded by God during the now dead and defunct Mosaical covenant.

2-15:15fl.—In a now familiar theme, RA cites Psalms 57:7-9 where the scripture mentions a "harp" in verse 8. He also states, and accurately so, that the original Hebrew here in verse 7 uses the word zamar which means; "give praise with a stringed instrument." The logic breaks down because RA, again, wants to apply a scripture that was addressed; "To the chief musician, Al-taschith, Michtam of David . . ." to us who are living in a NEW dispensation! Of course, if one were to ignore to whom the scripture was addressed and the dispensation under which the addressee lived, one "might" get the idea that it applies to us Christians today. The folly of this "logic" is best described by a verse RA cited earlier in the presentation, Exodus 15:20. In this passage, Miriam plays instrumental music in celebration of the fact that God had delivered the children of Israel safely out of the hands of Pharaoh and his army. This instance predates the Law of Moses. RA states that since God authorized, or at least allowed, the use of the instrument BEFORE the Law of Moses was given, He will now authorize, or at least allow, the use of instruments AFTER the law of Moses. As I have noted before, this all "sounds" good until things are taken to their logical conclusion. "IF" this logic holds true, we would be offering burnt offerings every Lord's Day. We would also purchase homes and cars by cutting animals in half, letting the blood flow in between the now sawn asunder animals and requiring all the parties to walk through the blood to "seal the deal." That's what God and Abraham did BEFORE the "law was given." (See Genesis 15) All this is why God says that the ". . . things written aforetime, were written for our learning," NOT for our obedience! Rightly dividing the Word of Truth requires us to, again understand, that "though the Bible is written FOR us, much is NOT written TO us!"

Sadly, at this point RA "seems" to infer that God should have "communicated" more specifically during the time between the testaments regarding instrumental music "IF" He wanted it removed in NT worship. He says that;

"IF" God changed His mind between the Testaments (regarding the instrument) He would have: a) Given us a clear passage condemning it's use, b) Given us a clear passage commanding a cappella only and c) gave us a prophesy announcing the end of the instrument in worship."

Why not take the Scriptures for what they ARE rather than what we WISH them TO BE? Why would we presume to argue with God because we don't "like" what He says and how He says it?! Our approach to the Holy Word MUST be this:

"What is God saying?" as opposed to, "What do "I want" to hear from God so as to suit me?"

Let's examine RA's logic. First of all there are MANY Old Testament worship practices that are not part of New Testament worship where there are no passages condemning their use! Not only do we not find any passages "condemning" instrumental music in worship, we don't find any "thou shalt not" passages regarding the use of incense and the wearing of priestly robes! Secondly, ALL New Testament passages that discuss music in worship refer to that practice as SINGING! [Many, though, as we are discussing now, want to find pianos, guitars, drums and trumpets "hidden" in the word "singing."] Finally, MANY aspects of Old Testament worship passed away without any specific "prophesies" announcing their end. This line of thinking is consistent with the Emergents desire to DECONSTRUCT and then RE CONSTRUCT the church. Clear and revealed truth is discarded in favor of finding "new and hidden truths."

Having exhausted his use of the Old Testament, RA now turns to the New Testament to "prove" that these radical departures from the scriptures are somehow warranted. Not only does he turn to the New Testament, he makes two of the most extreme points this writer has EVER heard from anyone within the church of Christ.

First of all, he asserts that instrumental music in worship is "acceptable" because Christ "never dealt with the subject in the gospels." It is a radical and dangerous misunderstanding of God's Word to "elevate" the gospels over the rest of the Word and here's why: 1) We KNOW that the ENTIRE Word of God IS the very Word of Jesus, THE LOGOS, beginning to end! By inspiration, John says:

> "In the beginning was the Word, and the Word was with
> God, and the Word was God. The same was in the beginning

with God. All things were made by him; and without him was not any thing made that was made."—John 1:1-3

When Jesus speaks, whether in the gospels OR through the epistles . . . ALL the words are the Words of Christ! ALL the Words are delivered and preserved by the Holy Spirit! 2) To say that since Jesus did not directly deal with this, or any other subject for that matter, in the gospels that this "somehow" devalues any other dealing with it elsewhere in the New Testament is simply wrong. Such a view relegates the Apostles and other writers of the New Testament to little more than "commentator" status. We KNOW, however, that Peter, along with the other Apostles, assert WITNESS status along with the HOLY SPIRIT when it comes to speaking for Jesus as we see clearly in Acts 5:32. It is the view of this writer that these same two witnesses are one and the same as the two witnesses of Revelation 11:3-12 who of them is said; "And I will give power to my two witnesses . . ." This is very serious business. To say that "some" truth is "more true" than "other truth" is a claim of "higher knowledge." One would have to possess this "higher knowledge" in order to decipher between "lower truth" and "higher truth." My friends, if this is not Gnosticism, it is Gnosticism's first cousin.

Secondly, RA asserts that instrumental music in worship is acceptable since when Jesus cast out the "money changers" in the temple, he did not cast out the "musicians." I must respond with the painfully obvious; the musicians were there because God Himself ordained their presence! This cannot be said of the moneychangers, they were cast out. The interpretive methods that would draw such a conclusion of "acceptability" of mechanical music in worship are so shallow as to defy measurement. Today, there is no temple, there are no money changers and there is no instrumental music in God approved worship! God operated DIFFERENTLY before Christ than He does today! As Gentiles, we were "outside the tent" before Christ. NOW, we are "under Grace and NOT under Law." Praise God! Let's not retreat back to condemnation!

I would now like to address another assertion RA makes during this point in "Both /And" Lesson 2. He asserts that the ONLY passage in the New Testament that addresses the subject of corporate congregational singing is I Corinthians 14:26. He "claims" that NEITHER Ephesians 5:18-19 and Colossian 3:16 are references to "corporate" or "congregational" singing. However, what do these two texts actually say? Let's look:

Eph. 5:18-21: "And be not drunk with wine, in which is excess; but be filled with the Spirit; speaking to *yourselves* in psalms, and hymns, and spiritual songs, singing and making melody in your heart to the Lord, giving thanks always for all things to God and the Father, in the name of our Lord Jesus Christ; Submitting yourselves one to another in the fear of God." (Emphasis mine, RM)

Col. 3:16: "Let the word of Christ dwell in you richly in all wisdom; teaching and admonishing *one another* in psalms, and hymns, and spiritual songs, singing with grace in your hearts to the Lord." (Emphasis mine, RM)

The word rendered "yourselves" in Eph. 5:19 and "one another" in Col. 3:16 is the SAME word! It is the Greek word; heautou. ***Strong's*** says this concerning *heautou;*

"(*Heautou* is) from a reflexive pronoun . . . (of) him, her, it, them [in *conjunction with* (Emphasis mine, RM) the personal pronoun of the *other* (Emphasis mine, RM) persons."]

To see how the translators addressed *heautou* in both passages I checked 9 different versions via *e-sword.com* and my own personal library (KJV1611, KJV, NKJV, YLT, ESV, Websters1828, Douay-Rheims1899, ALT and ASV). Colossians 3:16 is universally rendered either "one another" or "each other" by all 9. Ephesians 5:19 is rendered either "each other" or "one another" by the ESV, ASV and the NKJV. The rest of the versions render it "yourselves."

It appears clear to this writer that the word "yourselves" is a plural word in a collective setting. It is NOT a *CONTEMPLATIVE* term! There is something afoot in the religious world today CLOSELY associated with emergent theology called "Contemplative Theology." "Completive Theology" is totally self centered and self directed. It is Eastern in its origin and mystical in it's application. It is, in fact, Gnostic. "IF" Paul had a completive meaning in mind he would have said; ". . . speak to YOURSELF." "Yourself" is a singular word, "yourselves" is a plural term.

Why have I spent so much space on these two verses? Simply this, RA would have us to believe that these passages refer to one's DEVOTION (alone) and not one's PUBLIC WORSHIP (collective.) The use of the COLLECTIVE and PLURAL word *heautou* can ONLY refer to a public, corporate, collective and plural worship experience! While it is true that I Corinthians 14:26 refers to corporate worship, Ephesians 5:19 and Colossians 3:16 ALSO refer to a public, corporate, collective and plural worship experience!

In one last attempt to make his point, RA cites James 5:13 *in conjunction* with Ephesians 5:19 and Colossians 3:16. As previously established, the latter two passages are clearly referring to a corporate, public, collective and plural worship experience. James 5:13, however, can be viewed as referring to an individual and devotional setting. However, he ignores the text and the context of both the Ephesian and Colossian passages and "forces" his James 5:13 interpretative template onto and into the text and context of Eph. 5:19 and Col. 3:16. . . . . Round pegs and square holes . . . . In lumping these three passages together, RA states that;

". . . all (3 passages) "clearly" address the individual. The corporate assembly is not the context of any of these 3 verses."

This is an example, in the view of this writer, of how one can use circular interpretation to link disparate passages together to support any kind of pre conceived theological conclusion.

Blending ingredients is for the kitchen, not the pulpit.

2-30:32—At this point, RA turns to the *Revelation*. He cites two passages, Rev. 5:8 and Rev.15:2 & 3.

Rev 5:8 "And when he had taken the book, the four living beings, and four and twenty elders fell down before the Lamb, having every one of them harps, and golden vials full of odors, which are the prayers of saints."

Rev 15:2 & 3 "And I saw as it were a sea of glass mingled with fire: and them that had gained the victory over the beast, and over his image, and over his mark, and over the number of his name, stand on the sea of glass, having the harps of God. And they sing the song of Moses the servant of God, and the song of the Lamb, saying, Great and marvelous are thy works, Lord God Almighty; just and true are thy ways, thou King of saints."

I would like to quote what RA says on two occasions regarding these two passages. These quotations speak for themselves.

"Is God enjoying in heaven right now what He is despising on earth?"

"I do not believe that God is going to hand you a harp after sending millions to hell for mistakenly playing one."

With all due respect, RA here seems to ignore the most obvious of all facts regarding the *Revelation*. That is the fact that the *Revelation* is written almost entirely in figurative language. To take these passages literally will soon take us into the camp of the Pat Robertson's of the world looking for the so-called "rapture" and the "1,000 year reign." The first verse he quotes here illustrates my point. "IF" the "harps" are literal, then so would be the "golden vials full of odors." However, the text CLEARLY states that the "golden vials full of odors" ARE the prayers of the saints! The passage is clearly metaphorical and not literal. To say, then, that the "harps" are literal and that the "golden vials full of odors" are figurative . . . such discernment would have to come from a gift of "higher knowledge." Unless we are going to embrace Gnosticism, we must reject this line of thinking.

One final comment here on this section. RA seems to paint a picture here of a kind of "Jonathan Edwards Sinner's in the Hand of an Angry God" type of deity, not the God of John 3:16 who gives His only begotten Son . . ." RA sarcastically infers that God's judgment is arbitrary and capricious. Nothing could be further from the truth for, "The Lord is not slack concerning His promise, as some count slackness, but is longsuffering toward us, not willing that any should perish but that all should come to repentance." (II Peter 3:9—(NKJV) It is sad to say but RA's use of theological sarcasm is certainly one of the many low points in these 3 sermons.

Scriptures Regarding Worship & Partaking of the Lord's Supper on Saturday

3-6:19—RA begins this section by citing Acts 2:46:

> Acts 2:46-47: "And they, continuing daily with one accord In the temple, and breaking bread from house to house, ate their *food* with gladness and singleness of heart, praising God, and having favor with all the people. And the Lord added to the church daily such as should be saved."

RA opens this section with another example of circular and multiple meaning interpretation. He ignores both history and language in order to arrive a conclusion that is not even part of this text. His conclusion is that this passage allows for worship, with communion, as being permissible on Saturdays.

First of all the context of this passage has to do with the very first congregation of God's people. The uniqueness of this congregation was never duplicated again as far as we know. This congregation was a TEMPORARY one in many ways. It was a congregation made up of a substantial, possibly a majority, number of the dispersion. (Acts 2:5-11) Most of them returned in a matter of months and those that did stay were soon scattered by persecution. (Acts 8:4) This first congregation DID, in fact, meet daily. Included in the "daily" is, of course, Saturday. This congregation did meet on Saturday for; ". . . they, continuing daily with one accord in the temple, and breaking bread from house to house . . ." Prior to the church being outlawed and persecuted, she met daily in the temple courts AND from house to house. However, once persecution and the scattering came, the "meeting daily" aspect of Christianity was not transported elsewhere and we have no records of such EXCEPT for this one congregation born under the most unusual of circumstances. The daily meeting in the temple courts was used as an opportunity to preach to large numbers of fellow Jews. (Acts 3:9fl) The daily meetings in the homes were primarily for fellowship AND the partaking of common meals. This is how thousands of people were fed while in a foreign land many weeks journey away from their homes. In addition, it was simply not possible for Gentile churches to meet daily since a large portion, perhaps majority numbers, were made up of slave populations. Slaves would not have the freedom of daily movement away from the masters quarters.

3-7:51—RA gets only ½ of the history regarding time correct. At this juncture, RA asserts that; ". . . . Jews did not keep time like us, the Sabbath begins at sundown." The southern and urban Jews, living in and about Jerusalem, did in fact count time this way. However, the northern rural and agrarian Jews living in and about Galilee . . . including the apostles . . . reckoned time with the day beginning at SUNRISE. We know this as a certain fact for Peter says in Acts 2:15 that he and the 11 could not be drunken for; "it is but the third hour of the day." This would have the apostles Pentecost sermon at 9:00 a.m. "IF" we take RA's assertion as a reality, Peter and the 11 would be speaking at 9:00 p.m., making a "not drunk at 9 p.m." statement unbelievable and unreliable, if not laughable. The misapplication of the historical record here is the basis for RA's argument ongoing: "Since some of the Jewish congregations reckoned time with Sunday beginning at 6 p.m. Saturday night . . . our time . . . then we can scripturally worship on Saturday nights." (My words RM) This line of thinking is so circular as to stretch credibility.

3-10:35—At this juncture RA misapplies and quotes out of context Romans 14:5 which says; "One man esteemeth one day above another: another esteemeth every day *alike*. Let every man be fully persuaded in his own mind." He asserts that each of us should "follow our own convictions" as to what day to worship since, as the text "says," no one day is to be esteemed over any other day. With very little effort we can clearly see that Paul's subject here in this text is FEAST DAYS and not which day to WORSHIP! Again, the thinking here is so circular it's like going to Chicago from Charlotte via Honolulu. He concludes this portion with this quote which speaks for itself: "Choose the day that is consistent with your conviction and your worship preference and your calling from God." A Hindu could say AMEN! to such a statement.

3-12:51—In an amazing attempt to justify communion on Saturday, RA asserts that the term "breaking bread" in Acts 2:42 means "communion." In other words, the 1st congregation partook of the Lord's Supper daily, according to RA. He further asserts that EVERY instance of the term "breaking bread" from Acts

335

2:42 on universally means "communion." As mentioned earlier (3-6:19), the "daily" meetings were unique to the Pentecostian congregation in her infancy. However, daily meetings were never intended to be a "pattern" for all other congregations henceforth to utilize. There is absolutely no scriptural, historical or patristic documentation for such a claim. The term "breaking bread" in the N.T. is interchangeable, based upon the text and the context, between common meals and communion. Also, in a similar vein, RA asserts that ALL Lord's Supper commemorations were held as part and parcel of the Love Feast in 3-13:38. This was the practice of the Corinthian congregation for Paul wrote to them in I Corinthians regarding their brazen abuse of the practice. Like daily meetings for common meals and fellowship, the Love Feast was an early practice that historically soon faded. RA does great disservice to biblical interpretation by taking these two early 1st century practices by transporting them to the 21st century and then parachuting them into an entirely different time and culture, finally misapplying them in such a way so as to justify our meeting for communion on Saturday! Such a misapplication must rest in the "hidden messages" in these passages now "discovered" for the very first time by Rick Atchley. As mentioned several times in our study, the pursuit of the mystical and the unknown are far more important to the Emergent church than the pursuit of clear revelation, the truth that is both verifiable and obtainable. [For a more complete examination of both "breaking bread" and the "Love Feast," see Everett Ferguson's article in Austin Graduate School of Theology's *Christian Studies* vol. 21 pgs. 21-38 entitled; "Lord's Supper and Love Feast."]

3-19:23-21:31—In an effort to show that the time to partake of the Lord's Supper was carte-blanche freedom of choice, RA turns to I Corinthians 11:23-26 and Revelation 11:6. He asserts that the original word translated "as often" (hosakis) gives us all the freedom to partake of the Lord's Supper ANYTIME we so choose! He bases this thesis on D. A. Robertson's definition of (hosakis); ". . . is only used with the notion of indefinite repetition." (***Grammar of the Greek New Testament in Light of Historical Research***, pg. 973) This IS the sense of Revelation 11:6 for this passage speaks of figurative future events to be brought about by the figurative "two witnesses" as God brings judgment upon the Roman Empire and her false religion of emperor worship. However, that is where the similarity ABSOLUTELY ENDS. When we examine I Corinthians 11:23-26 in it's PROPER CONTEXT, we discover that Paul is relaying the words of Christ to His apostles during the Last Supper. It is therefore, both linear and logical to ask the question; "After the church was established, how did the Apostles interpret the "often as" statement?" In other words, WHEN did the Apostles partake? What example as to when to partake did they leave us? Knowing that "Scripture interprets Scripture," we find the answer in Acts 20:7—"And upon the first *day* of the week, when the disciples came together to break bread, Paul preached to them (ready to depart on the morrow) and continued his speech until midnight." This SHOULD end the discussion but RA asserts just prior to this section in 3-19:02 the following:

"The pre-eminent text that we have used in churches of Christ for years to prove that you can only have communion on Sunday is about a church that has communion on Monday."

To "discover" such "new revelation" in these texts is beyond this writer's imagination, which by the way, I never apply to interpretation of scripture. First of all, the text SAYS that they "came together to break bread" on the "first day of the week." The first day of the week is Sunday. Corinth was in the Roman Empire. They kept time according to the Romans. How did the Romans calculate time? Simply put, like we do, from midnight to midnight.

338

Sunday ended at midnight! *(beaglesoft.com/timehistoryroman.htm)* The Corinthians, because the text so states, had the Lord's Supper BEFORE Paul preached! The only way to conclude that these brethren partook of the Lord's Supper on Monday . . . after Paul's discourse . . . is simply speculative fiction. There is nothing in the text, there is nothing in history and there is no patristic evidence to support such a fantasy!

D. The "Both/And" Sermons Ignore or Re-Interpret Clear Apostolic and Patristic History

There are more than several instances in the above section that cite the shredding of both Apostolic and Patristic history. In addition, note the following:

2-6:38—Quote: "I contend that you give this Bible to any sincere person with no preconceived conditions and say; "Just read it (the Bible) and find out what God wants of you," that no one just reading this Bible would conclude that using instrumental praise is unacceptable to God." [Authors note: I suppose that RA does not consider Luther, Calvin, Spurgen *et al* to be "sincere persons." Clearly he is ignoring the historical record in his assertion.]

Even more incredibly, RA continues even further into his historical denial:

2-46:01 (MOL)—Quote: "Thousands have studied the Bible INTO using the instrument and NONE have studied it OUT of using the instrument." [Authors note: Has RA never heard of Campbell and Stone?! This is as incredible as North Korea calling itself "democratic!"]

3-7:51—RA incorrectly asserts that ALL Jews kept time from sundown to sundown. We have already proven, by Peter's statements on Pentecost, that the Northern Jews (those from Galilee) kept time from sunrise to sunrise! He fails to cite any reference for his assertion.

3-8:43—RA asserts that EVERY New Testament worship service was in the evening to allow slaves and the poor to come. While it is likely that MANY worship services were held at night, there is NO PROOF that ALL worship services were held at night! Again, there are no references to back up his assumption! Night or day, the Lord's Supper was taken after midnight Saturday and before midnight on the Lord's Day. It was NEVER taken on a Monday until the Roman apostasy had taken hold.

3-9:49—RA asserts that Jews worshipping at a Gentile congregation would ALWAYS be meeting on Monday morning. As noted above, there is no reference cited and no proof given for such an assertion. There is nothing in either the historical or patristic record to even suggest such an idea.

3-13:38—Here RA asserts that the "love feast" enclosed around the Lord's Supper was the universal, permanent and biblical pattern for the sacred memorial. There is not a shred of historical or patristic evidence to support such fantasy. The practice ceased just a few years beyond the establishment of the church. The extreme abuse of the practice by the Corinthian congregation gave the practice very bad press, as it were. For a detailed review of this topic, see Everett Ferguson's aforementioned article in 3-12:51.

3-14:07—In a bold and reckless way, RA here states emphatically that the early church held communion EVERY day! Thus, we can partake on Saturday and be in God's Will, in his mind. I have covered this assertion previously in 3-12:51. There is absolutely nothing biblical about such a teaching.

3-14:17—To "support" his assertion that the primitive church celebrated the Lord's Supper daily, RA "says" that "church history" supports the assertion. His documentation? He says that a group of so-called "church fathers" (Patristics) claim such. It all sounds very plausible to an audience that may not be quite up on ancient history. He rattles off quite the list; Cyprian, Ambrose, John Chrysostom, Basil and Augustine. What he FAILS to do is to disclose WHEN these men actually lived! ALL these men lived when the church was in free fall apostasy towards full blown Romanism. Here are the facts:

- Cyprian was born in 200 and died in 258.

- Ambrose was born in 340 and died in 397.

- John Chrysostom was born in 347 and died in 407.

- Basil was born in 329 and died in 379.

- Augustine was born in 354 and died in 430.

Who were these men? They had one thing in common . . .

Error.

Cyprian, Chrysostom and Augustine crafted and enshrined the transubstantiation heresy that claimed that the bread and the wine of the Eucharist became the LITERAL body and blood of Christ when blessed by the priest. Ambrose was ordained and installed as a "bishop" BEFORE even being baptized! During his tenure he began using the power of the Roman church to influence politicians by first threatening and then carrying out an order of excommunication against the Roman emperor Theodosius. Basil created the monastic system to train celibate monks and nuns for Rome.

It is the words of THESE men that RA cites as "proof" of every day celebration of the Lord's Supper. In one sense he is right, the 3rd and 4th century apostate church DID, in fact, celebrate the Eucharist daily! However, the 1st century church of Christ DID NOT!

I have used as sources for this section the following:

—Dates of births and deaths: *answers.com*

—For information regarding Cyprian, John Chrysostom and Augustine, I cite:

F. W. Mattox, *The Eternal Kingdom*, Chapter 12—"Life, Worship & Doctrine Under Romanism," Gospel Light Publishing Co. 1961. pg. 149-159.

—For information regarding Ambrose and Basil, I cite:

F. F. Bruce, *The Spreading Flame*, Chapter 34—"Five Leading Churchmen" and Chapter 35—"The Monastic Life," Eerdmans 1992. pgs. 329-341 and 342-352.

E. The church of Christ is Continually Spoken of in Semantically Un-Kind Language.

These statements, unfortunately, speak for themselves. I will make not any further comments.

1-49:49—"The church of Christ is just a part of the Kingdom of God. They're not the entire Kingdom of God."

1-50:21—RA says he stays at Richland Hills ". . . to free people from the slavery that has been imposed on them." (i.e. the teaching of the Scriptures)

1-55:36—RA states that he is "tired of (the church of Christ) being known for what we are against."

2-6:38—In regards to the instrument in worship, RA says; "I realize now that that conclusion (that the use of the instrument is wrong—RM) was simplistic, it was judgmental, it was arrogant and it was divisive."

2-30:32—In regards to the use of the instrument in worship, RA says; "Is God enjoying in heaven right now what he is despising on earth?"

2-40:50—In regards to those of us who adhere to the truth regarding the use of the instrument in worship, RA says; "(Our theology) (is) . . . a deeply flawed way to read the Bible, it is inherently inconsistent and it is inevitably divisive."

2-48:24—"We are creating a very serious credibility gap for we don't even any longer defend what we practice."

2-50:23—"God does not segregate life to the point that what is acceptable in a car or in a wedding is not acceptable in a worship service."

2-50:33—"I do not believe that God is going to hand you a harp after sending millions to hell for mistakenly playing one."

2-50:40—"A God that would love me so much that He would die for me would send me to hell because I did not properly understand something that He never spoke about?"

3-22:49—"There are many in our heritage who are still struggling with placing faith in a plan more than a man . . . They are looking for a pattern of doing church that they can duplicate. It's a salvation strategy with a track record of producing anxiety and division and tremendous inconsistency."

3-23:24ff—"It's because they've (you and I that have remained faithful RM) believed a false gospel. It's a gospel that says that if I don't get every detail right, not just the details that God made clear, but the details He didn't make clear. If I don't get inferences and silences right my eternal soul will burn in hell forever. And if that is your gospel, you are going to be anxious, you're going to be fearful, you're going to be angry . . . . Everywhere it's preached churches split and churches decline and children leave . . . it is an affront to the Gospel that if you don't get it all right you will burn in hell."

3-38:10—"Our task is not to duplicate these earliest churches. Our task is to imitate their goal of being culturally relevant outposts for the Kingdom of God . . . . Let's admit that all churches make cultural concessions to reach our neighbors."

3-46:39—"I know the Kingdom of God is larger that churches of Christ but is the heritage where I was raised."

CONCLUSION TO THE APPENDIX

I have presented the truth in love regarding these matters. In that spirit, it is the biblically arrived at conclusion of this writer that Rick Atchley's "Both/And"[230] sermons draw erroneous conclusions from Scripture, are based on flawed logic, misinterpret the historical and patristic record and thus render the teaching, in it's collective totality, FALSE.

—Russ McCullough/Charlotte, NC/June 6, 2008

---

[230] "What will be the end of it all? It may well be that a new creative provocateur in the Kierkegaard mold will step into our midst and write another *Either/Or*. This one may call it ***BOTH/AND***. The point is that diffusion tends to create confusion, and confusion within a culture creates vulnerability."—Dave Breese, 1990

BENEDICTION

"May the God of all grace and mercy allow us to see a time that we all will lay aside our opinions to seek only Thy will in all our ways for the sake of Jesus Christ our Redeemer, our Lord and Savior and the Head of His church forever and ever through whom we pray." Amen.

Russ McCullough/Charlotte, NC/June 6, 2008

GENERAL WEBOGRAPHY

Listed in Order of Reference

Answer.com—www.answers.com

Wikipedia.com—www.wikipedia.com

ReligiousTolerance—www.religioustolerance.org

Authors Sinners Prayer Website—www.sinners-prayer.info

Lower Hudson Blogs—

http://religion.lohudblogs.com/2007/01/22/what-makes-one-an-
  evangelical/

Aspiring Theologian Blag—http://aspiringtheologian.modblog.
  com/

Authors Biblical Interpretation Blog—

http://samuelslinesaulscircle.blogspot.com

Christianity Today—www.christianitytoday.com

Brian McLarens Website—www.emergentvillage.com

United Methodist Church Nashville—Brian McLaren Quote

www.archieves.umc.org/interior.asp?ptid=2&mid=9040

Emergent Report on PBS—www.pbs.org/wnet/religionandethics/
  week845-and-pbs.org/wnet/religionandethics/week846

Wade Hodges Blog—http://wadehodges.com

Northwest church of Christ—Shoreline, WA—www.nwchurch.net

Richland Hills church of Christ Website—www.rhchurch.org

Crosspointe Christian Church, Ashland, Ky. Website—
www.crosspointecc.us

Dave Miller's Article, "Is Baptism a Symbol?" from Apologetics
    Press—www.apologeticspress.org/articles/2285

Evangelical Manifesto Website—www.evangelicalmanifesto.com

Kinetic Christian Church, Charlotte, NC—www.kineticchurch.com

Providence Road church of Christ, Charlotte, NC—www.prcoc.org

STADIA—www.stadia.com

Provision Ministry Group—www.provision.org/

Church Development Fund—www.cdfonline.org

NND.COM On Line Articles—www.nndb.com/Origen

Arsdiputandi Theological Jourrnal—www.arsdisputandi.org

Tim Castle's Blog—http://timcastle.blogspot.com

"Out of Ur"—Christianity Today blog—http://blog.christianitytoday.
    com/outofur/archives/2007/03/goodbye_religio_1.html

Song Lyrics—www.lyricsfreak.com

Song Lyrics—www.oldielyrics.com

Ozark Christian College—Website—www.occ.edu

Tulsa International Soul Winners Workshop Website—www.
    tulsaworkshop.org

ZOE Group Website/New Wineskins—www.zoegroup.org

The Berean Beacon—www.bereanbeacon.org

Understanding the Times—www.understandingthetimes.org

Phil Wilson's Blog—http://jphilwilsonsblog.blogspot.com

United Religious Initative—www.uri.org

Allan Jones Grace Cathedral Website—www.gracecathedral.org

Mecklenburg Ministries (Mecklenburg County, Charlotte, NC)—

    www.meckmin.org

Pew Research Poll on Religious Preference—

http://religions-pewforum.org/pubs/876/religion-america-part-two

Pepperdine University—www.pepperdine.edu

Greg Taylor Blog—http://gregtaylor.cc

Lipscomb University—www.lipscomb.edu

Leafwood Publishers—www.leafwoodpublishers.com

Extreme Theology—http://extremetheology.com

NOTE: No endorsement from the author is expressed or implied by these postings. Always remember to "test the spirits!"

SELECTED BIBLIOGRAPHY

Allen, C. Leonard & Swick, Danny Gray, *Participation in God's Life*, (Leafwood Pulishers. Abilene, TX) 2001

Allen, C. Leorard; *Things Unseen: Churches of Christ In (and After) The Modern Age* (Leafwood Publishers, Abilene, TX.) 2004

Atchley, Rick & Russell, Bob; *Together Again*, (LeafWood Publishers, Abilene, Texas), 2006

Benedict XVI, "Origene: il mondo, Cristo e la Chiesa," tr. it., Milano 1972, p. 43. (Homily On Origen of Alexandria. Vatican City. Zenit—April 25, 2007)

Breese, Dave, *Seven Men Who Rule the World from the Grave*, (Chicago, IL., Moody Press, 1990) [I would like to thank Bro. Terry Wheeler for giving me a copy of this book! "Thanks, Terry!"]

Carson, D. A.,"The Emerging Church." *Modern Reformation Magazine.* "Faith a La Carte?" (July/August 2005 Issue, Vol. 14.4

Deist, Ferdinand, *A Concise Dictionary of Theological and Related Terms* (Pretoria, South Africa: Van Schaik, 1990, 1992)

Foust, Michael, "Max Lucado Transcends Church of Christ Beliefs," in *Baptist Press News*, May 9, 2005

Ferguson, Everett, *Church History, Volume 1—From Christ to Pre-Reformation* (Grand Rapids, MI.:Zondervan}, 2005

Haroutunian, Ellen, "A Baptism of Imagination—A conversation with Peter Kreeft," *Mars Hill Review* 5 (Summer 1996): pgs. 56-73

Jackson, Wayne, "The "Pope" Ignites a Controversy," in the *Christian Courier*, July 17, 2007

Jones, Alan, Reimagining Christianity-Reconnect Your Spirit Without Disconnecting Your Mind: (Hoboken, New Jersey: John Wiley and Sons 2005)

Kaiser, Walter C., *Toward an Exegetical Theology—Biblical Exegesis for Preaching and Teaching*, (Grand Rapids, Michigan: Baker Books. 1981, 2006) Chapter 2: "The Definition and History of Exegesis"

Kaiser, Walter C. Jr. and Silva, Moise's, *Introduction To Biblical Hermeneutics—The Search for Meaning*, (Zondervan, Grand Rapids, MI, 2007)

Liddell, Henry George and Scott, Robert, *A Greek-English Lexicon*, 9th ed. (1940), I, 690,

Marian, Lynne, "Conversations Count: An Interview with Brian McLaren," *Outreach Magazine*, July/August 2005.

MacArthur, John, *The MacArthur Study Bible*, (Thomas Nelson, Inc., Nashville, Tennessee}, 2006

McGrath, Alister E., Christianity's Dangerous Idea—The Protestant Revolution—A History from the 16th Century to the Twenty-first, (New York: HarperCollins, 2007)

McLaren, Brian, *A Generous Orthodoxy—Why I Am a . . .* , (Youth Specialties Books/Zondervan, El Cajon, CA. and Grand Rapids, MI., 2004)

McLaren, Brian, Everything Must Change—Jesus, Global Crises, and a Revolution of Hope: (Thomas Nelson, Inc., Nashville, TN., 2007)

McLaren, Brian and Ortlund, Anne, The Secret Message of Jesus—Uncovering the Truth That Could Change Everything, (W Publishing Group, Waco, TX, 2006)

Mickelson, Berkeley, *Interpreting the Bible*, (Grand Rapids, Michigan: William B. Eerdmans Publishing Company. 1963, 1977) Chapters 1 & 2: "Source of the Interpreter's Principles" & "Lessons from he Past"

Miller, Ph.D., Dr. Dave, "Is Baptism a Symbol?" *Apologetics Press*, On-line journal article, 2003

Nestle Greek Text with a Literal English Translation Copyrighted as Literal English Translation by Samuel Bagster and Sons Ltd. 1958 and contained in: The R.S.V. Interlinear Greek-English

New Testament (London: Zondervan via Samuel Bagster and Sons, Ltd., 1968, 4th printing, 1972)

Osborne, Grant R., *The Hermeneutical Spiral—A Comprehensive Introduction to Biblical Interpretation* (Downers Grove, Illinois: InterVarsity Press, 2nd Edition 2006)

Pharr, David R., "Antioch—A Church of Christ—Acts 11:19-30," *Carolina Messenger,* March, 2008

Pharr, David R., "What it Means to be Distinctive," *The Spiritual Sword* 39 (January 2008)

Robinson, Haddon H., *Biblical Preaching—The Development and Delivery of Expository Messages,*(Grand Rapids, Michigan: Baker Academic. 1980, 2001)

Ross, Bobby, "Survey: Americans See Many Routes to Eternal Life," *Christian Chronicle*, August, 2008, pg. 4

Schaeffer, Francis A, *The God Who Is There—Speaking Historic Christianity Into the Twentieth Century*, (Downers Grove, Illinois: Intervarsity Press, 1968, 1975)

Schaff, Phillip, *History of the Christian Church Vol. II*, (New York, New York: Charles Scribbner's Sons, 1883(?), 1910)

Taylor, Greg, "The 21st Century Restoration-Will We Join It?" *New Wineskins*, March-April, 2008.

Taylor, Rebel, "Max Lucado Shares Hope With Abilene Congregation," *Abilene Reporter News Online*, 17 February 2008

Various Contributors: "A Handy Guide to Church History," *The Spiritual Sword*, Volume 39: July 2008: No. 4

Vine, W. E., M.A. *An Expository Dictionary of New Testament Words with their Precise Meanings for English Readers* (Old Tappan, New Jersey, Fleming H. Revell, Company, 1940, 17th Impression 1966)

Wiker, Benjamin, *Moral Darwinism:—How We Became Hedonists*, (Downers Grove, Ill, InterVarsityPress., 2002)

Woodson, William, "The Danger of Modern Philosophy," *The Spiritual Sword* 39 (January 2008)

Woodson, William, "Who Wrote the First Five Books?" *The Spiritual Sword* 39 (October 2007)